SIDDHARTH ARYA

LIFE
after a
PASSING REMARK

NewDelhi • London

BLUEROSE PUBLISHERS
India | U.K.

Copyright © Siddharth Arya 2023

All rights reserved by author. No part of this publication may be reproduced, stored in a retrieval system or transmitted in any form or by any means, electronic, mechanical, photocopying, recording or otherwise, without the prior permission of the author. Although every precaution has been taken to verify the accuracy of the information contained herein, the publisher assumes no responsibility for any errors or omissions. No liability is assumed for damages that may result from the use of information contained within.

BlueRose Publishers takes no responsibility for any damages, losses, or liabilities that may arise from the use or misuse of the information, products, or services provided in this publication.

For permissions requests or inquiries regarding this publication, please contact:

BLUEROSE PUBLISHERS
www.BlueRoseONE.com
info@bluerosepublishers.com
+91 8882 898 898
+4407342408967

ISBN: 978-93-5819-004-5

Cover design: Aman Sharma
Typesetting: Namrata Saini

First Edition: August 2023

ACKNOWLEDGEMENT

So finally, here I am writing my first book, really excited, though nervous also on same time as I am still thinking what will I write which can fill pages good enough to have a book. Writing a page or two or three has been never a challenge for me but its altogether a different task to write a full book – hats off to all the authors in this world, who have written such amazing books and have given this world such stupendous literatures to read, grow and transform.

I am not able to recall exactly, when did I conceive this dream of someday writing my own book, but when I actually started thinking about it on serious lines, even then It took me long to prepare myself and go ahead attempting the one. And it took me long because for so many years, I was not able to actually accept my ability to write or rather I should say I was constantly avoiding that discomfort which we all go through when we attempt something new or doing something for the first time in life as the feeling of dealing with uncertain always makes us anxious. Also, I was avoiding it as there was fear of failure which I always used to feel as I was never confident about what should I write and do I even have something good to write about, because for me only those people should write or talk about their life or part of life who have achieved something significant as then only people can be inspired, but trust me every human being has a story to tell to the world which can leave impact on people and humanity.

Even while I have started writing, I am still little nervous that will I be able to deliver what I want to, through my book and touch people who are going to spend their hard earned money buying my book and spending their precious time reading it.

Year 2019 brought one of the darkest times for this whole world with the outbreak of COVID-19, which left this world never the same as past. Just one virus proved it to whole world yet again that life is and will always remain unpredictable. One virus changed everything for everyone around the globe and also taught us what should be given priority and importance.

During COVID-19 lockdown, people explored and discovered lot of new hobbies and interests. During those initial couple of months of lockdown in India, almost everyone became the cook and it can be proven by the weight gained by their family members (I am one of them, gained 5 Kgs during that time). Honestly, though it was tough time, but it also proved to be one of loveliest time for I and Shikha, my better half since 2013, as I and Shikha both are working, so we never got enough time to spend together, as our normal 9-6 jobs allowed us to see each other in mornings and then in late evenings only and on top of that Shikha had 6 days working, so we were only left with Sundays to be together. During that lockdown, we spent almost 2 months on home together, and first time in my married life I enjoyed being with her for whole day, whole week and whole month. I got opportunity to enjoy hot meals all three times of the day. One day I saw Shikha buying a blog space online as out of somewhere she decided to start writing blogs, so I enquired to her about it and she shared the whole process & cost. As usual, I again got an adrenaline rush and started visualizing what if I also starts writing a blog. I worked on it and started writing Hindi blogs. And I started with the thought that for a good time, I have been thinking of writing a book but never ever could I gather that much confidence on myself, so let's at-least start writing blog.

Anyways, I wrote my first blog and it was into Hindi with Title "Vicharo ka Mehatva" and I shared it to all my friends and family and received overwhelming response to it. Got lot of appreciations on the clarity of content, message and selection of words. It was yet again, when I thought of starting writing the book but same ending again – thought remained the thought.

It was a weekend evening and we were at my In-laws house. I and my brother in law were enjoying drinks with kids playing around. Shikha and her mother were sitting on bed discussing very important topic – what to be prepared in dinner. It was then, when my sister in law came to me and asked "Jijaji, the blog you wrote was copied from somewhere or you wrote it on your own", it took me a minute to answer as I was scared, hope I have not committed the crime of copyright infringement to some other blog. I replied that those were my own thoughts and she then asked me that I should start writing a book, adding I writes so well. Though the conversation ended as a passing one to me and I did not take it that seriously. But then same evening, Shikha was working in Kitchen preparing dinner and I was as usual lying on my single bed in drawing room watching TV (that was my most favorite pose at home), when suddenly a voice turned into my ears "Siddhu" .. I ignored the first one as I thought, it must again be some work in kitchen or home so better avoid it but she called me again and all married males can relate that you are not allowed to ignore your wife's call as it can have dire consequences.

"Siddhu - I think you should think seriously about writing a book" - Shikha said.

"Write a book and share your journey to people. Who knows, people might love it and also get to know of your journey and life as so many people must have suffered the same challenge as you did. But please make sure that it should not again just remain an idea, rather start working on it and get it published".

I just replied "Hmmm" - a sound human beings create to answer in situations where we do not have a clear response to give ie either Yes or No and we just want to wrap that conversation there only.

But that day, this conversation remained stuck in my head and especially when Shikha said that "make sure it just doesn't remains just an idea". COVID times had already showed that do whatever you want or dream to do in life, as no one knows how far you are from abyss, so don't restrict yourself from doing things you love or want. And I believe that pain of failure is always less than the guilt of not attempting and so from that day I actually started making content in my head, as to what will I really mention in the book, how will I start, how will I middle it, how it will be concluded.

Why I shared all this, because this book is not just outcome of my efforts or my writing skills, which have recently seen the big sky to fly and aspire to reach heights, but this book is rather the result of collective efforts of so many people out of my life and their belief and conviction in me which was many times more than I carry in myself.

Thanks to this Universe for giving me people in my life who have supported me in each and every situation and every dream of mine and who kept standing with me in everything. Thanks to everyone who embraced even my mistakes and flaws and helped me become a better person every day.

I dedicate this book to my First Love.. my daughter Anaisha as she is the one who gives me energy and intent to get out of my bed every morning and work hard to make life better and give myself and my family a life they all deserve.

Thanks to my parents first, my existence on this planet is because of them and whatever little I am today is all because of their hard work. I grew up seeing them working hard making the ends meet somehow and I realized this even more once I gained senses as even though there was always shortage of money in family, but what they never compromised on is giving us good education and values. Love you Mumma and Papa, my life belongs to you.

I thank my spouse Shikha as she has been one person always giving her best to make me feel special and make me believe that I can do whatever I want in my life – she has been a blessing to me because having a partner who always sees your potential and trust you more than you do yourself is just so wonderful. Life throws its own set of challenges and problems on you but it's always about the people you are surrounded with which determines the time you shall take to fight and bounce back.

Also, thanks to my siblings (Megha di and Ghanu) for always being there for me whatever the situation is, they are not just my siblings, they are rather my power pillars. Love you both.

And last but not the least, thanks to Umesh and Yatin bhai for their huge contribution in transforming my belief system and my conviction in myself. Their constant effort on helping me work on my mindset and thoughts and get evolved as a human being has really helped me transform internally and change my world inside and so do outside. Thanks Umesh, you have been such an amazing person and I am so blessed to have a friend like you in my life, whom I can reach anytime for anything with sheer trust that you are there for me.

Thanks to all those, who are not mentioned here but they have somehow touched moved and inspired me to do what I do and become what I am today.

PREFACE

In India, it is not allowed legally, but I got married at age of 15, not to a girl (no, please don't consider I am a gay and got married to a guy) but and I was married to my complexes, my inferiorities and self-doubts. I married this feeling of mine of always short of something and lack of abundance. I was so committed to my relationship with my partner that even if anything good used to happen, I used to doubt it.

I lost all my Self-love and started seeing myself as an unwanted member in my own family. Something changed inside me and that changed everything for me in outer world. I was afraid of being with more than 2-3 people at once and I always used to think like I don't belong to normal people and I am just a package of so many flaws – I don't look good and am I good enough for anything.

I started believing that I am a below average boy with nothing special in me and this became even more strong living in a family where everyone was so good looking and so talented be it my elder sister, my younger brother, my parents, my cousins (as we used to live in a joint family).

I started cementing my complexes with circumstantial proofs around me and started looking at me from this new outlook of mine about myself. I used to look at myself into mirror like there is someone else looking at me from the mirror with pity in his eyes and saying to me "OO God, who are you - you have no grace" and from here my struggles started of making myself a match with my family.

Unfortunately, there are so many friends of mine in the world who exactly feel the same way about themselves – little less or more, living their lives in shell, scared to come out of their world of self-pity, seal-beating and afraid of being among the people.

Lockdown due to COVID-19 did few good things too and one of it was re-telecast of Epic Ramayana.

Every morning, my wife's tilted eyebrows with a glance on TV used to reconfirm to me that I have again put the channel on DD National where I was watching Ramayana daily. Would like to confirm that daily here means morning as well evening.

In Ramayana, as Shri Ram was give the exile for 14 years by her mother Kaikayi and they started living in jungle along with Brother Laxman and wife Sita. The whole Ramayana happened as Sita ji was abducted by Ravana from their hut in jungle when Ravana came in face of a saint, leaving Shri Ram and brother Laxman aghast and from then Shri Ram was in search of her. This is when Shri Ram met Hanuman and then King Sugreev who was thrown out of his own kingdom by his real brother Vali who owned super human powers and strength. King Sugreev helped Shri Ram in search of Sita ji sending his army of apes in different directions. One such team having Jamvant, Hanuman, Angad and Neil were all standing on shore of Sea one day and were discussing who will fly across the this huge Ocean and will go to Lanka where Goddess Sita is anticipated to be kept. Hanuman in that scene was standing calm and quiet behind the Jamvant, ignorant of the fact that he was the son of the God of Air – Vayu and he has the inherent ability to fly effortlessly to anywhere in the world. Jamvant ji asked Hanuman to accept this challenge of crossing the Ocean flying and go to Lanka, to which Hanuman reacted like he has been asked to do something so beyond his reach and looked petrified or rather confused, as he was not expecting Jamvant ji to ask him to do the humungous task. And it was then the Jamvant Ji made him recollect who he is and what are his capabilities which he was made to forget in childhood, but once Hanuman was able to see clearly who he is and what he is capable of doing rest remained the History.

Purpose of sharing this here is to say that we all human beings are just like Hanuman. We all have all the powers and capacity to do and achieve anything in life but either we are not known to what we can do or we do have the whole world full of doubt over ourselves.

All we need in our life is one person or one situation which makes us aware of what we are capable of doing and what we can accomplish in our lives and sometimes this one person or one situation ignites the fire of transformation inside us and leaves us as a completely different person altogether.

We all just need one Jamvant in our life who empowers us and make us believe our self and realize our potential and powers. Sometimes, our Jamvant is hidden inside us only and sometimes in face of someone else and we need such one Jamvant in our lives who can give us direction and convert our speed into velocity. For those, who doesn't clearly understands the difference, velocity is nothing but speed with direction and this is so profusely required to grow as just keeping speed and no direction shall takes you to nowhere in life majorly.

Till this moment, lot of us keep living our lives like ordinary people who are there out in world only to survive with no belief in themselves that they can also do something extra-ordinary and can somehow inspire others by causing a difference first in their own life and then others.

I was also no different and used to even think that successful people are different people, they are lucky, they have inherited money, they are born talented - Yes a few are but not all.

Since long, there was always a discomfort inside me, a restlessness of doing something remarkable in life, a restlessness of becoming someone from no one - a person on whom I myself can be proud of - a person who when sees himself in mirror pats on his back and says WOW - I have lived my life the way I wanted to.

A restlessness of accomplishing my dreams and also the dreams of my parents who have lived their whole life struggling to make the ends meet and for whom it is now my responsibility to cause a life of abundance and happiness.

But then ...

There was this tiny internal voice which always used to give resistance to my confidence over myself, over my dreams, over my aspirations and over my self-esteem. A voice which kept telling me that I am not good enough, I lack something in me, I cannot do anything big in life, I don't look good, People don't love me and almost everything which it could have to make me feel small and incomplete.

And it was this internal voice only which kept me away from whatever I wanted to do or attempt in life – be it personal, professional or social. It took away my self-love which took away my relationships with others and most importantly my relationship with My Self.

It took away my ability to acknowledge be it other's accomplishments or mine, be it good things happening around me or I causing the good things around, be it my efforts to make life better or others helping me become better, be it the things I should be grateful for or the challenges which were making me a better person every day.

But, I was not born this way. I must have come to this world like all other kids who comes to this world carrying all the innocence, love and excitement of doing wonderful things, the kids who are being joyful, happy and lovable and living their life with lot of self-love and self-respect. In fact no kid comes to this wonderful world with any kind of inhibitions, any kind of complexes or complaints neither about them nor about any other person or object. Kids are the purest and best form of Humans who do not carry any judgement, any incompletions rather they just carry love, compassion, forgiveness, curiosity and no fear towards anything or any person or any situation. Kids have a different dictionary in which there is no spaces for words like Failure, Despair, Fear or Rejections.

But then what start happening to us with time, while we grow in terms of age and our senses as lot of us start losing our self-love and compassion and we start carrying so many fears, inhibitions and complaints about ourselves or other ones. We starts disbelieving us and lose faith in ourselves, our capabilities, and our potential and begin to live life inside shell wasting our so precious Human Potential.

I lived my life this way for almost 15 years and when I got present to the source of this being of myself, I discovered a new ME. A new ME, who wasted so many years of my life doubting, complaining myself & never accepted the person who has been living inside me since I was born.

So here, I invite you to walk through the journey of my life and attempt to discover, to understand what shapes us into what we are today and do we really have access to change or transform this old being of ourselves and create a new YOU who can live a life with self-love and love for others, who is complete in himself and has no complexes around him or world, someone who has respect, love and compassion for all including himself and who always carries high self-esteem. This book is my journey from that day of one incident which changed everything inside me and so do outside in my world, to the day when I had that level of esteem and confidence in myself which took me in direction of a decision of writing and sharing with everyone what happened and what it did to me and my life and how it started for me to realize that I am not what others think of me and even not what I think of myself.

From being someone what I shared in lines above to becoming someone who now believes that I can do anything, who now loves himself, admires everything about himself, takes every criticism as an avenue to improve or at least do not takes it personally and someone who is now ready to take on every challenge and willing to work the heart out to grow and evolve and create around a world of Love, Harmony and Affinity.

This transformation was not quick & easy but it was worth it because it made me understand the person living inside me and it made me understand that I am also born with each quality a person needs to grow and become successful and if there is something I do not have, I can learn and enhance.

This transformation gave me belief and conviction in myself and my abilities. It gave me confidence and the power to acknowledge my flaws and mistakes and also my accomplishments without considering them fluke.

But what actually happened, what changed the course of my life downwards and what helped me emerge back and altered my thinking and perspective about myself and my life. And how my sharing can help my readers see their lives from a point from where they can also get present to the fact that Why they are the way they are? Which can give them also the access to the Awareness and Transformation, the access to know the Real YOU - So, I invite you all to let's go further on this roller coaster ride ...Bon Voyage !!

CONTENTS

Chapter 1: What Happened 1

Chapter 2: Career and Work Life 17

Chapter 3: Relationships 26

Chapter 4: The Breakthrough 45

Chapter 5: The Rise 72

Chapter 6: How to love yourself 81

Conclusion 94

CHAPTER 1

What Happened

So, let me start sharing a fictional story here..

This story is about a village of Frogs, a village which was located inside a deep well in some remote area of a small town. The well was no more used for any kind of water supplies as there was not much water left in it.

In this well, there used to live some families of frogs – there were mumma frogs, daddy frogs and baby frogs. They all used to watch the sky from inside the well, every morning turning beautiful blue then getting yellow during daytime and then dark in night with glittery stars shining all over and it was really fascinating for all as the frogs have no idea of what it is and why it keeps changing colors in every 3-4 hours, sometimes they were scared while other times it was fun for them just sitting ideal and watching it, as for them, it is something out of their world - The Well. It was ages, all these frog families had been staying there in well and no frog ever tried to go out of well and explore the world, for whatever reason had been stopping them be it uncertainty or the age old conditioning that we are born to live this way.

An evening, some kid frogs were playing while they see another kid frog trying to jump high and get out of well and discover the outside world. The other kid frogs looked at that kid frog with surprise as they had no idea what he was attempting and when they understood, they started telling him that jumping out of this well is not possible and he should not try this as few other frogs also tried this in past but either ended as failures or died attempting.

The baby frog did not listen to them at all and continued trying jumping as high as possible and go out. He tried going back to one end of inside wall, take a stance, run and make another jump putting his little feet on wall and in this whole attempt, he fell down so many times hurting his legs, his back as the ground inside the well was stony with small pebbles and stones scattered over everywhere.

The other frogs kept making fun of him but the baby frog did not give up.

He looked at all other frogs standing apart, laughing, shouting and took another stance, ran down the stony runway and jumped high putting his little feet on one spot then another and disappeared out of the Well in a flash. All other frogs standing there were shocked and surprised as no one was able to believe what just happened – this news percolated in the whole village, that a tiny little frog jumped out of the Well. He did something which no other frog has ever done and whoever heard about it, the reaction was like "Are you kidding", "not possible" and so on. Some other frogs also started saying that the frog must be god gifted or he might have attended some special classes or training for doing that, family support must be there and bla bla bla .... There were feelings of jealousy, deprivation and criticism all over with some mouths even praising the courage and effort of little frog. In evening, all frogs of the village gathered together in the ground to discuss – how did he do that ?, and so finally an experienced, aged frog suggested to go and meet the mother of baby frog to understand if there was something special in him as he did what no other frog could ever do.

All frogs reached the house of the little frog. A muddy hut made with mud walls & the roof made of dry brown straw. In the front courtyard, there were 3 stairs that takes you to inside the house. Sitting on the stairs, his mother was crying as she was concerned about her son being out of well now and all alone. All frogs and families gathered at baby frog house, and they all tried to console her and some of them also started asking various questions – was he a special kid, was he given some education or training for that, how could he do that etc etc. His mother somehow managed to control herself and said that she has no idea if her son was any special or not, but he was deaf from the birth and could not hear anything and that's all she told to all the frogs gathered there.

Story ends.

You all might be thinking, first why I shared this story here and second what a boring end to story, nothing interesting or exciting, so allow me to answer them both.

You know why the baby frog was able to do what he did?

Because he was deaf and fortunately as he was deaf, he could not listen to anything which the whole village was trying to tell him which is "You cannot do this" or "No one has ever done this and this is not possible" and as he did not listen to all this, so while other frogs were laughing and shouting at him, it was only occurring to him like, other frogs are encouraging him and supporting him to go and do what he wanted.

No words could reach his head and thus no person, no situation, no failure was able to condition his mind and tell him what is possible and what is not. As he could not let any suggestions or remarks or comments enter his brain, thus there was no little voice inside his head telling him - YOU CANNOT DO THIS and thus his mental conditioning was not allowed to be intoxicated by WORDS. He had no idea that there is something called Failure or Fear and so he continued attempting and ultimately made it possible not for only himself, but now for so many others living their life inside the Well and who were completely cynical about moving out ever till this happened.

Why I shared this story here, we all are like these frogs only – we keep living in our own well – safe, secure, protected and certain and sometimes spends our whole life there. And not because we actually do not have the potential to jump out, but we have been rather made to believe that we do not have the potential of jumping out or breaking out the boundaries and cause something different is not possible, reason being the people around or we ourselves or the situations but ultimately what matters is what are we believing.

I believe and hope you all will agree that each and every kid in this world is born free of any limits, carrying no judgements or inhibitions either about himself or anything or any person in the world. Every kid is born only with love, compassion, curiosity, excitement and no fear.

It is when a kid starts growing and see people around, listen to and watch his parents, family, and friends and go through different situations of life, there he starts picking experiences, opinions and starts forming his thought process, mindset and identity. This whole process is run through our Subconscious mind and so it is really automatic. It is actually the world around the kid that shapes his personality and character and with whom he starts looking at the world, at himself, at every situation of life, at every relationship and at every incident.

The traits of our personality are not given to us by birth, rather by the experiences we have gone through and most importantly what behavior of us or our near ones got us out of that situation and helped us save ourselves or our reputation as our brain validates those actions or behaviors and store them for recurrence in future for any similar situations, as the prime objective of our brain is our Survival.

I was also no special and must have been carrying no such apprehensions or inhibitions about myself or others, but it was that one single day which turned things for me, it was that day when that one passing remark was made on me and it changed me and my life negatively for a pretty long time.

As far as I could remember, I must be 15 at that time and it was a bright sunny day and we were all at residence of a relative as it was some ceremony there. My uncle had built a nice big 3 storied house in a posh sector of the town. It is kind of house which a common man always wants to own in life, a big house with a parking and a small lawn outside with main gate having a wooden name plate, entering from main gate you reach the outer lobby which was studded with high quality black and green granite with cheque design on floor, on one side of which there was entrance to the living room which was big room with three side sofa sets and a beautiful centre table in between. Walls were having texture paint which was another attraction for us to see as we only had normal paint on our walls in home, so seeing it was like seeing something extraordinary. On one side of the drawing room, there was a beautiful TV Panel built with branded Veneer polished with natural wood lacquered polish, under which they had their Pooja Ghar. You all must be thinking why am I giving a detailed description of all this, but trust me, all this was like a dream interior setup for us back then in 1998-99. And to add to it, they had a Voltas Window AC in their drawing room, which was like super luxury and only rich people having lot of money could afford it.

It was some function at their house and as the event ended quite late, we all stayed at our uncle's house only. Next morning, everyone woke up late, we all cousins were just enjoying having couple of rounds of tea and matthi & namakpaare (one of the most common snack item kept in bowls on dining tables those days). It was around 11 in morning as all of us were sitting in drawing room. Uncle was sitting on one of sofa placed alongside the wall, in his shorts (this was his most favorite place and pose) with my parents sitting on another sofa discussing something with my tauji and taiji, wherein I and my sister were having tea and bread pakora (one of my favorite breakfast option, especially when served with jaggery sauce). Some other relatives from uncle side were also there having breakfast as after attending function last night, now all were planning to leave for their homes. Kids were actually not enjoying that discussion as we all just wanted to be together for some more time and not go home too early. These are those times when your parents look like dictators to you and you pray to God to make you grow up fast so that you can take all your decisions yourself.

The room was full of people, some chit chatting while other discussing when to leave and someone discussing the food or arrangements of function and leaving all this apart, I and my cousins were only focused on finishing the pakora in our plate and getting just one more, like pakoras on planet are going to end.

It was when the heavy and bassy voice of uncle fell in my ears, while I was busy enjoying pakoras, it took me a moment to get it, what he was saying.

Uncle: Nawal (my father's name), is he your son really – Siddharth?

At first I was not able to understand what is he saying and I gave that reaction too looking at my uncle face and giving him a look like someone has asked me something in French and I am as versed with French as a chicken is with taste of omlette. I could not understand, what was he asking, as surely I am my father's son, while I was confused, he continued.

Uncle: Who does he resembles to? Doesn't look like part of this family.

He continued talking to my father – "Look at yourself, what a handsome man you are and look at him. From nowhere, he looks like your son" and he said all this carrying a witty smile on his face as if like he was enjoying making fun of me and my appearance.

I had no idea, what he was referring to and his persistence on the question made my face turned blank and a confused pause replaced smile on my face. I felt really bad, really insulted and embarrassed, think of a teenager who was punished publicly just for being not so good looking or not having an appearance matching his family. I felt like why am I here present in this moment and was feeling really small. Everyone present in room reacted differently to this comment of my uncle on me, my cousins laughed, my parents were neutral may be they actually had no idea how and what to respond to this sudden remark from him considering a very respected position is hold by husband of family's daughter in Indian families and they are generally not confronted or retorted back. Some looked at me giving me a look like they second the thought of my uncle and saying to me silently that your uncle is right and you does not match your family as everyone in my family, be it my father or my mother, my elder sister, my younger brother, my cousins, they all were very good looking, very fair but somehow I was not but till this moment in my life I was never present to this fact or maybe I should say that I was never ever made present to state of my looks so harshly by anyone and in presence of so many people and with no one standing by my side and countering my uncle and giving me a support which could have given me power to fight that situation and not let the conversation impact me and my life for such a long time.

It was my first ever encounter with social embarrassment or criticism on my looks or presence and as far as I can recall, it was the day, the moment when I unknowingly picked some traits of my character and made lot of decisions about how I need to live and what I need to do in order to avoid any such recurrence of execution of my grace, dignity and respect.

Tough to even understand the mindset of a 15 year old teenager, who was about to enter one of the most important phase of life, where he must have planned so many things to do and might have dreamed of so many achievements and accomplishments and becoming someone from no one to change the life of himself and his family, a family who has struggled for a long time but somehow never compromised on giving all the basic things a child deserves and needs. But that one moment, that comment from my uncle, left me so incomplete about myself and the reaction of all others in room made me really small in eyes of my own self. In that moment, I felt like saying to God that please do some magic and disappear me from this room and take me away from this moment - a moment which inculcated a whole world of inhibitions, apprehensions and complexes inside me and from then I started behaving and living each and every minute of my life being someone who doesn't looks good and who doesn't belongs to his own family and his very own people.

That one comment from my uncle gave birth to another human being inside me, another Siddharth who was always there to remind me that I do not look good and I do not belong to my people.

I started sleeping with that comment, waking up with that comment, eat with that comment and carry it everywhere I go and everything I do. I used to look into mirror and reinforce that comment into my subconscious though unknowingly as it was all automatic and without I knowing that I am doing it to myself. I started hating myself and thus I also started disliking everything which was good looking or anyone who looks good as to me the source of criticism to me was the people with good looks as due to their presence only I am compared and not comprehended. My relationship with my own self was getting deteriorated and so do my real relationship with others too.

There is something called Self-concept.

It is nothing but what you think about yourself, what you tell and say about yourself and how you feel and what you believe – who you are.

This self-concept determines how well will you do in your life, how well will you do into your relationships and how you will sustain or handle them. It determines how you will treat others and how others will treat you, it determines how you see yourself and how you see the world because the outer world for any human being is nothing but the reflection of his inner world and how one's inner world is, depends on what the person thinks and how and what he relates himself to – that inner voice which keeps telling us always and which resides inside us every moment – our self-concept determines what it will say to us and how we are going to act and behave in any situation of life. Your results are determined by the actions you take, your actions are determined by the thoughts you pursue and give relevance to and your thoughts are impacted by your theory about yourself because how you see yourself deep inside, that's how you think and relate the whole world to be and that's how you approach, talk and behave to anything or anyone. So much literature has been written on Self-love by so many amazing, great and successful people. You can find hundreds of wonderful books on loving and accepting yourself because it is the only access to you to provide that required acceptance to your internal being which then allows your being to work on itself and improve on any possible area of life and once you starts working and shifting your being – everything starts shifting. You are the epicenter of your life and your world and for your world to change, it needs you to change and confront whatever is not working in your life and see what you can do about it because you are the cause in the matter of everything that happens in your life, consciously or sub-consciously.

In that moment, when I encountered that comment from my uncle, my self-concept immersed deep down and it went so down that it removed the self-love from my being and created a void which was filled gradually with disbelief, feeling of unabundant, deprivation, low esteem and then started coming many more such experiences and situations which all strengthened my belief that I LACK SOMETHING and I AM NOT GOOD ENOUGH, not because world was telling me that, but rather I was only listening that, it was like the radio of my mind was set to that specific frequency wherein only one and one channel was showing up.

My uncle made that comment on me only once, but from that moment, that internal voice inside me started repeating that comment to me every day & every night. I used to wake up with that thought and I used to go to bed with that thought, like a recorded message has been played in loop. Every time I used to see or meet anyone with good looks, I used to corner myself from him / her and people around and go into a shell. I started having another person residing in me which was only and only criticizing me. As this universe always gives you what you believe into and that's what I started believing that I am not good enough and hence the Cosmic Law started working against me. And while I was still trying to absorb and understand completely what is happening in my life and the source of this drastic fall in my confidence and energy, I encountered another incident of criticism on my appearance, re-affirming to me that I seems like an odd one out in family.

My parents have always been part of cultural as well social groups though my mother was more social than father. She was part of a kitty group also, wherein every second Saturday of month, she used to go at place of some member of her kitty group and some 20-22 women used to be there and play games and enjoy food and have fun. Once in a cycle, it was done at our house also and that used to be the day of feast for us. Samosas, Pakoras and other snacks with soft drinks and tea. Preparations used to get started from morning itself with cleaning of house and moving beds and sofa to one side of lobby to make space on floor for matting as all used to sit down on floor only and start the episode of laughter and fun.

Though the group was big, but there were some 3-4 aunties which were really close to our family specially my mother and also kept coming at home, as they all were elder to my mother, we kids used to call them Taiji (term used to address wife of your father's elder brother). Our childhood has been a struggle in terms of finances as father's business never worked well and mother started working as a teacher in a local school so somehow we could manage things but one thing which our parents never missed on, in-spite of having almost no money, was enjoying time and having fun with us.

Yes, the level of fun was different, there were days when even calling a dinner from just a small dhaba and that too just simple Dal and Tandoori Roti was fun for us or maybe going to market together and eating golgappas from a desi thela or going to Gangaji with one of the cultural group of our parents where we would just go and take bath in River Ganga enjoying fruits and matra chat, but mummy and papa took great care of that we should be spending and enjoying small small moments together and I think that laid the foundation of togetherness in beings of all of us three kids.

It was one such trip to Rishikesh with four of aunties from my mother's kitty group and our whole family. Husband of one of aunty was also with us in trip. We stayed in a Dharamshala (kind of a charitable trust) and it was such a memorable trip as we really enjoyed roaming in local markets of Haridwar and Rishikesh. Eating lunches and dinners on dhaba, wherein you can feel the taste & aroma of tandoor & coal on roti and that smoked flavor in dal, basic chopped onion and cucumber in salad but trust me there is no replacement for this food, no matter you go and eat in an elite premium restaurant or a five star hotel.

In Rishikesh, we were at Triveni ghat taking bath in Ganga and enjoying Mangoes dipped in cold river water of Ganga in a jute bag when I heard something. This time, though the comment was not made directly at me but the subject was myself. One of the aunty from group was standing close to my mother and was saying something to her. We were all wet standing half dipped in water on stairs of Triveni Ghat Rishikesh, the weather was pleasant and surrounding was serene as till wherever you can see, it was beautiful greenish Ganga River flowing, touching mountains on both sides. Ghat (bank of river) was full of people and saints who were wearing Saffron Chola having long beards, curled hairs and wearing Sandal teeka on forehead that too big enough covering almost whole forehead.

I was really playful and enjoying when that remark landed in my ears and in a flash of moment it took me back to my familiar world of confinement of my complexes and inferiorities. Things occurs to you differently when you already have a perceived notion about something and that's what was happening with me also.

I heard aunty saying to my mother – "Siddharth looks little different in your family. Doesn't resembles much to you or his father".

Though this comment could have been taken positively also by me as being different is not always bad, people who have been different only have been able to accomplish amazing things, but this is how it works, when there is lack of self-esteem and self-love inside you for yourself, you relate every incident, every event to your own personal shortcomings and failures.

In that moment when I heard aunty saying that to my mother, this time I was more disheartened because I felt helpless and hopeless in terms of like – Do I have to live my whole life like this now, getting criticized about my looks and appearance, am I bringing shame to my parents or family, have I become a source of jest here. I was ungrateful and was angry to God, why am I the way I am and if this is how I have to be then why am I being born as child to the parents who looks so good. I had deep disappointment in me as I had no idea what should I do to overcome this or end this for me and my family. As a son, I just wanted to be like my father, my family, and my people and see that appreciation in eyes of others which I generally used to see for my other family members. I was deprived.

And this feeling of deprivation, this loss of self-love, confidence, lack of self-esteem and unhealthy self-concept, started impacting each and every aspect of my life. What I started carrying for myself was only anger, frustration and deprivation and it changed the occurrence of everything to me, be it any person, situation or relationship. Your response to anything in life depends on how it occurs to you and so does my response to my life itself started getting negative. How?

CHAPTER 2

Career and Work Life

Tell me, who are the best Salesmen in world?

Are they the one having best knowledge of product they sell - not necessarily? Yes, the knowledge of your product, your services and your organization and industry is vital to know and it helps you win the Customer's confidence in you and your company and product, but just having knowledge doesn't makes you the Best Salesman.

Are they the people who are really good looking and smart or handsome. Like knowledge, it might be surely a positive influencer in making Sales but not the factor that decides Sales.

Are they the people who speaks fluent English, good at presentation or communications? Again, these traits can be helpful but not the deciding factor in your success in Sales.

So what is that one common trait or personality of all those Superstars in Sales be it in a Job or own business. That is High Self—esteem and a very positive Self-concept. Studies have proven that people with high self-esteem and positive self-concept are best in Sales because they carry lot of belief, love & respect for themselves and so they do for others also. They do things with conviction which gets transferred in their eyes, voice and gestures and it influences positively the other person, which helps people winning other's confidence and also the Sales.

And when I talk about Sales here, I am actually not only talking about Sales as a function in any company or Organization, I am talking about Sales on a very broader perspective where it is not just about selling a product or service, it is rather about everything you do in life because Sales exists in each and everything we do. Be it talking to someone, be asking or giving anything, be it doing your own work, be it seeing a girl or boy for marriage or dating, be it asking your boss a increment or promotion, be it negotiating with a vendor in market, be it parenting or anything. Every time you open your mouth to speak anything – you are selling something. And people do not talk, they share their beliefs and opinions, they talk what they believe and so every communication is actually a war of belief systems and whichever belief wins actually wins the game or conversation or customer or situation.

Why I shared all this is because what kind of Salesman you become in life majorly depends on what you think about yourself and how you see yourself ie How is your Self-concept.

People with high self-concept are not feared of failures or rejections or NO's in Sales, because they relate themselves high and they know that no rejection or NO is for them – it is only for their product or service offered and that too not permanent and thus they are not impacted badly by any amount of rejections or failures and they keeps going. Their Self-concept is so strong that no rejection brings down their Self-esteem and when your self-esteem remains high, your brain keeps generating good hormones which pushes you to do more and stay happy and excited and this excitement gets transferred to other people and finally they gets influenced to buy from you.

Happiness is directly linked to our feeling of accomplishment & competency and when your self-concept is high and strong, you keep generating results and this keeps adding to your Happiness which in turn adds to your Self-concept which in turn again makes you work and take actions with excitement and cause results. So, if you can see this is a cycle which keep repeating itself and gives you Success in whatever you do and not just only in area of your work but rather in all areas of life. Be it health, relationships, finances or your social life because people generally wants to connect and stay with Happy Souls only.

In contrast to this, when your self-concept is low, you doubts yourself and belief in your actions is found missing. You are feared of failures & rejections as you consider them personal. If any customer says No to your offering, you do not take it as NO for product or service, rather take it as NO for yourself, like customer doesn't likes you and that's why not buying from you and this ends the future possibilities of you approaching that customer again, so with people with low self-concept, it is very tough for them to approach same customer again and even if they do, their own brain keeps telling them that this customer is anyways going to say NO and which eventually happens most of times as the Law of Universe works in sync with your clearing of thoughts and emotions.

Negative self-concept doesn't just reduces your Sales – it reduces your overall capability of generating results, be it any area of life, because you move into anything with doubts, lack of confidence and low self-esteem and with such an attitude, it is almost inevitable that results shall not be caused.

Negative self-concept impacts your Self-love because you start disliking your own self and starts comparing yourself with each and every one. When there is no self-love, even small criticism ends up to you like a humiliation because it lands personal to you. Lack of self-love constraints you from appreciating and acknowledging others because you have no acknowledgement and appreciation for yourself and so it becomes tough for you to do it for someone else, which starts shaping you as not so good team member and a bad team leader because to work with people, you have to learn acknowledging them. With no self-love, you always carry this feeling of deprivation and lack in your life and thus you generally do not appreciate abundance in other's life which never allows universe to give abundance to you – because Universe always gives you what you appreciate and acknowledges.

On that day, when my uncle left that comment on me in front of so many family members / relatives in their own house, it initiated my separation with my self-concept and self-love and as I started living that comment every day in my mind, this separation only and only got strengthened and I had no idea when it started becoming my reality. A reality which made me a boy average in all areas of life. This process was so automatic and I bought this with so much of conviction that I used to sell it to myself every day that whatever he said was right – I am actually not good in anything.

This impacted my growth in my career also. I was always a bright student but in my graduations my marks fell down substantially and I couldn't score even 50% as aggregate in by Bachelors. I was so immersed in my complexes by the time I turned 18-19 that I couldn't dream of doing any good thing in life as there was always this sound from inside that "Siddharth, you are not born to do anything extraordinary. You are just an average common person and you do not deserve any Success in life". Post that incident, I started believing that people who becomes successful in life are different and I am not one of those. My subconscious programming got altered and it altered the blueprint of my life. I kept telling myself internally even before attempting anything that I will lose and so were the results most of the time.

And when you think like this, your whole body exhibits the similar frequency, you walk with bent shoulders, low confidence, your voice does not carry conviction and belief, you carry no spark in eyes and thus results also comes at same level.

Actually, more than fear of failure, it was the fear of embarrassment that if I could not do or present or perform anything rightly, people will make fun of me, they shall laugh over me because that incident left me scared of being public anytime, because for me - if I shall be among people, they may make laugh of me anytime, so even if I used to be among people, my presence was minimal always. I never used to come in front or speak on anything in order to avoid being Public or exposed or visible to people.

And all this impacted my growth in my career very significantly because there is one thing which is common each and every where ie People. You be part of any company, team, organization, group or family – it's all people and people and people and if you are afraid of connecting and talking with people only, your growth can be tarnished by your own trait. When two people meet or connect or talk, their conscious beings only connect not more than 5 %, what connects rest is our subconscious beings and this process is so automatic that most of the times people are not even aware of this fact while outcome of any communication or conversation majorly depends on what is going inside a person and the another one. What are we carrying in our mind while getting in to meet a person or a group and in my case because it was always a feeling of non-abundance, a feeling of I lacking on something, a feeling of incompleteness, a feeling of I being inferior, so I used to only carry my full body physically there but the spirit was never taken along into anything and so every single cell of my body used to emit the energy in correspondence to my belief and allow me to not being present anywhere fully mentally.

So many instances, when I was admired or appreciated for something but it used to occur to me like Sarcasm as I was pretty confident about my incapability of doing anything good or even if sometimes I could feel the authenticity in appreciations given to me, my inner voice immediately used tell me that it's just a fluke and not your competency or efficiency. To myself, I used to occur as a person not normal and rather a person who is born to live a life of low profile. Someone, who is not deemed fit for anything remarkable, anything significant, anything big and this tyrannical mindset towards me was not actually from anyone else but from the person living inside me – Me, Myself and that's why every day it was becoming more and more stronger and ultimately became so strong that it barred me making any productive choices in life. I only started doing things where I can survive in shell and a zone of my own self.

After completing my schooling, I thought of doing Diploma Course in Software followed with MCA but till this time I had become a person who used to convince myself even before attempting anything significant that it is not for me. When I was trying to find a job for myself, a one on one interview was still OK but if there used to be any GD or Debate part, I used to abscond from interview just to avoid being part of group. I tried my best to find a job for me where I don't have to sell anything, where I do not require to come in front of people for anything. I used to get anxious if there is any role given to me where I have to lead people, give any presentation or speak to any group. Speech anxiety or public presence fear is normal and lot of people suffer from this but in my case I was not just hesitant of it rather scared of it and this is the effect that day, that incident left on me and my mind, my body, my life, my self-esteem, my self-concept, my confidence and left me a person who was a firm believer of his incapability. I could feel something diminishing inside me, like the light going off, the sun setting.

That's what one passing remark can do to you and your life. It can create a big distance between you and your own self and to accomplish anything significant in life, these two have to be ONE – You and Your SELF.

So here I request everyone who have spent their hard earned money to buy and read my book – please take on this Promise to yourself today that we will be accountable and responsible with our words as your words has the POWER to make or break someone. Words are not just words, they are the energy transferred using the language and right energy can do wonders to the faith, belief, relationships, love, affinity, harmony, environment, your surroundings, well-being and this whole world and vice versa unfortunately.

This does not just applies to when are talking to people at work, office, any social gathering but also at your home, while talking to your kids and family. Right words spoken to kids can open the world of possibilities to them, can make them believe in themselves and in this world and everything, while using words inappropriately in front of your kids, can tarnish their future and their beings and their relationship with themselves, the world and everything and every person because they see the world through their parents till the age of 5-9 specially.

So, be careful with your words because your word creates your world and many a times other's too.

CHAPTER 3

Relationships

Inside all of us, their lives another person, a person, a being, a soul who is present there every minute, every moment, living with us, sleeping with us, eating, laughing, enjoying, travelling to wherever we go. We carry him or her to every single place we go, to every single person we talk we meet we sell we present and so thus how will be our relationships with people out there in world completely and fully depends on how is our relationship with the person living inside us ie our self. If our relationship with our self is not healthy and strong, it will surely reflect in our other and every relationship. In our childhood, we all were taught by our family, parents, teachers that we should respect and love others and we should carry compassion towards all human beings and I hope every parent or family teaches this to their kids, be it any language or religion, but what has been missing since all ages is that you must be the first person in this list of others and you should first and foremost love and regards yourself. No one ever told us that being respectful, being caring, being graceful is not just required while treating others, but it is equally and rather more important, that we respect our self, we become caring towards us and we love our self. Our parents are also not wrong because they were also never exposed to this thought process or this way of thinking by anyone and like the rituals and ethics are passed on from one generation to another, the ignorance of keeping love towards yourself and being respectful towards yourself was also getting passed from generation to generation.

And when you do not love or respect yourself, it is almost impossible for you to love others because when there is love for yourself inside, it does not let your self-esteem and confidence go down even in tough times and when you are abundant inside, with no complexes, no feelings of deprivations or jealousy – you remains always open to acknowledge the good in others, you can whole heartedly admire other's accomplishments and your acknowledgements always lands and occurs authentic to others and with pure & sincere acknowledgements, it becomes easy to win people and their trust and make them like you. For example, when you acknowledge your wife for the good food she makes, it gives her energy to make better food and serve you with more love, when you acknowledges your team in office for their efforts, they give their best to put in more efforts as a team, when you acknowledge your kid for being a good kid or being good in studies, it gives them more encouragement to do better and all these acknowledgements helps you make people love you and like you more and so your likeability quotient keeps growing.

Self-love even allows you to embrace and accept gracefully your flaws and you gain access to turn them into your strengths. That's how loving yourself and accepting who you are gracefully allows your relationships also to flourish because you connect with everyone heart to heart and people around can feel the warmth in your presence and being. When inside, it is love, respect and warmth for yourself – it shows up into your voice, your eyes and your overall personality and it makes you a charismatic person over all.

Trust me – to be loved by all, start loving yourself. Wake up every morning repeating silently – "I Like myself, I Like myself, I like myself", say it before you going for a meeting, an interview, a date or anything important. Go to bed every night repeating same and just visualizing the version of yours which you dream or aspire to be.

***

Relationship with my brother

I have been really fortunate to have my childhood spent among lovely 5 families living together in a big ancestral property in our native town called Hapur, a small town in UP state. My grandfather had five kids, three son and 2 daughter and our grandfather's brother who had three kids ie two son and one daughter and so in total five brothers used to live in the big 300 square yards ancestral property which was built double storied. In one half of the property, used to live my Tauji & Taiji with their two kids 1 son & 1 daughter, our family ie my parents along with their three kids ie my elder sister Megha didi, myself and my younger brother Ghanu and on ground floor were my chachaji and chachiji with their three kids, one son & two daughters.

Evenings used to be full of fun, play and masti as we all kids used to group up in courtyard of house and play so many games like chuppa chuppi (a rural version of Hide & Seek), pakdam pakdai (catch me if you can), kho kho – a game where in team used to sit with alternative faces showing opposite directions and one person used to run while other had to catch him and the guy running to catch the other person can pat on anyone's back to swap and sit and let that person run and catch the guy. All elders used to sit and talk also and from there we initially saw and understood the idea & culture of Group Discussions. It used to be a jamming session of so many activities and discussions that when parents used to ask us to leave and get ready to go to bed, we would hate them.

I was seven when we got another member in our family ie my younger brother Paritosh aka Ghanu. My sister was 10 as I and Megha di had a gap of three years between us. Though I was not at an age of understanding anything then, but all I could remember is mother being admitted to Hospital and couple of evenings, I also went to hospital along with one or other elder family member carrying meals from home & it was like an activity of fun for me. So good were the childhood days, we could easily find fun in even the smallest and most of the irrelevant things

I still remember, one afternoon my grandfather asked me to come along to Hospital and I denied as I was busy playing with my cousins, so he asked me again and I denied again but then his perseverance gave up and landed in form of some 2-3 tight slaps on my soft cheeks and back then in 1990 it was more than sufficient for a kid to give up stubbornness and listen obediently to elders though halfheartedly.

Ghanu when born was super duper beautiful and cute. He was so fair that even on kissing him little hardly, his cheeks would go red, and his curly hairs would give him such innocent and cute look. Whoever used to see him would only and only showers the words of compliments, adoration and appreciations. I was so happy to have such a cute little brother. I still remember the day of his ear piercing (Karna Chedan), he was dressed up by my mother in a white and green dress with a white cap on his head and he was looking super beautiful.

My younger brother was a god gifted child as he has got the sense of music by birth. My mother used to give him boxes in kitchen while she used to cook and he could play the rhythmic music out of those boxes and from there we could see his god gifted talent to play any instrument which later in his life he proved too by having played any instrument given to him. My father used to and still plays harmonium (Indian piano) and he also tried getting me learn Tabla but I think I never had it in me to learn the Instrumental though I always loved singing and I still do. Having a son who has by birth talent of knowing Sur and taal and can play rhythm even on plastic boxes really made my father happy and later we also provided Ghanu tuitions for Tabla and bought Drum sets also for him.

All this never occurred wrong anywhere to me anyhow but after that incident at my uncle's house, having faced that criticism in front of all my loved ones which annihilated my self-esteem and confidence, something changed my relationship with my younger brother also. Gradually, I started seeing him also as one of the reason for I not getting enough love and attention in family and this is because he was so cute and good looking and I have already started accepting that I do not look good and also that all love and attention he is getting is because of his physical appearance and good looks. Now, whenever anyone used to come home and appreciate or show love to Ghanu, I used to feel bad, jealous and deprived.

I incessantly started looking for opportunities and chances where I can find his faults and make him appear wrong in front of family and parents. I did beat him so many times on his small & tiny mistakes, just projecting them to be big and bad. My insecurities grew up with time as he started getting more attention everywhere due to his artistic personality and capabilities, he was good at dance, music and drawing attention everywhere while I was so succumbed into my own world of complexes that my fear of facing people and connecting with them was growing at compound pace.

Gradually, my complexes and insecurity started to be with everyone who was good at looks, people loving and anyone who gets love, acknowledgements and appreciations from others. I won't name the people but trust me, the list was long. This is the power of one moment in life, this is what one passing remark can do to you, your life, your relationships, your mental health, your surroundings, your personal space & life and your career. We all takes our words so lightly but words have the power of changing one's life either ways.

With time, when we both grew up and I used to see brothers having strong bonds and relation, playing together, enjoying together, having a drink together, talking about girls and sex and careers, I used to miss having same relationship with my brother and trust me, whole life, it was never nothing wrong from my brother's end, he is a gem person and have always been such an amazing brother, even today, but it was always me who had no courage to go and talk to him and break that wall of complexes which has created an invisible gap between us. Acceptance of your shortcoming or mistakes takes a lot of guts and courage because you need to confront yourself and this becomes really hard if you are dealing with crisis of self-love and your self-esteem is low. People with high self-esteem and self-love are always good at accepting their mistakes because they know that making mistakes is part of life and they do no self-beating and start fresh. They do not narrate to themselves that "I am not good enough and that's why I keep making mistakes and it's better to give up attempting" and this becomes the source of failure for them.

And the same trait kept stopping me to talk to my brother and though we both were always together but not really together and like two real brothers and rather like two people who are just living together in one house.

***

My personal relationships

Teenage or Puberty, the one of the most exciting phase of every human being's life. A phase where so many changes started coming into our overall body, physically and mentally. One thing which is common in each and every human being is the cycle of life, no matter where you are born, which culture or religion you follow, what values you have been passed on, what color or caste you belong to, but you have to go through various cycles of life and Teenage is one of such phases of life cycle.

When our body reaches a certain stage, our brain starts releasing a specific hormone called Gonadotropin releasing hormone. This GnH (short term) on reaching our Pituitary Gland makes our body generates or release another two hormones Luteinizing Hormone and Follicle Stimulating Hormone and it further works on human body depending on our Gender ie works differently on bodies of Boys and Girls.

This hormonal changes in our body do something magical as the world around starts occurring different and colorful to us. Teenage brings a different kind of energy and excitement, even an eye contact with a girl or a guy gives you an adrenaline rush and immediately surrounding becomes colorful, air becomes breeze of fragrances and its blossom everywhere, you starts liking romantic Bollywood songs (LOL). Teenage or Puberty is altogether a different phase of life, where you gets introduced first time to the feeling of attraction, love and affection. Energy is always high and friends & friendship becomes integral part of life. You enters the phase where you want to take control of your life and doesn't any kind of restrictions or boundation.

I was also no different and was going through the changes teenage brings to your body, mind & heart (lol). I had also started feeling that excitement seeing girls. Must have been experienced by lot of us, when many a times we want to approach any girl, talk and strike the conversation but your courage or lack of confidence stops you. Sometimes it's also the pressure of being beaten up publically as it generally happens specially in Tier 3 cities, where you have to think ten times before approaching any girl as anytime you could be caught by nearby standing so called cousins or brothers of the girl and then they would give you all the love and blessings but through a different treatment. Another exciting thing is that in such cases when a guy is caught by girl's family or relatives or friends or cousins, every single person passing by turns out to be known of the girl's family and does not leaves without blessing you either with few packets of love loaded with some spanking.

I had friends who could approach any girl or talk to them quite easily and I also witnessed lot of relationships getting started just by having guts to strike a conversation with the girl, but in my case I was always scared or afraid of going and talking to any girl, even though I could sense her interest. Every time I tried going and talking to a girl, I used to feel anxious and could feel butterflies in my stomach, because back of the mind I always carried this thought that when I am not able to appreciate myself, how will she do and so I could hardly gather any courage to talk and share my feelings. And trust me guys, any proposal offered in love, business, family or life is surely going to fail or be rejected where the proposer himself is fumbling, lacking the confidence, conviction and self-belief. People who suffer with lack of self-esteem and self-love keeps generally struggles in proposing anything because they always have this fear of being said NO to and being rejected and for them the NO, the rejection is not for the proposal but rather for them as if like the other person doesn't likes him personally. Now this sharing or this part about my personal relationships might occur funny to many of you that I was not able to talk to girls easily, but I would like to invite you all to understand the deeper context of this sharing that what was the actual source of this problem. Let me ask you, if you have pure gold or lot of money or real diamonds or anything which is really precious, valuable and worth it and you have to offer it to someone, will you feel less in confidence or will you think what if other person makes fun of me or any fear of public embarrassment or insult – might be NO, because you deep inside knows clearly that whatever you are offering is of really valuable, precious and worthy. Now when we propose someone for a relationship what we are actually offering is US ie I myself is the Product offered and that's why when we do not consider ourselves Precious or Valuable or worth it, we have doubts or low confidence offering us or proposing us to someone.

For me, it was the impact of that incident that left me fazed in each and every aspect of life. I could hardly approach any girl because it was this strong persistent fear inside of getting embarrassed and getting laughed at and I kept failing to sell myself or my proposal to any girl. It was that resentment inside that when I am not accepted gracefully by my own people, should I even try acceptance from someone I don't even know. Trust me it was not fact that my people did not love me or accept me but that one incident at my relative house left me interpreting so many stories that I lost all my love for myself, all my respect for my own self and all my compassion for my own being. I was so deeply sad inside that it started showing up as the glow and grace on my face started getting faded.

Even when people used to like me or compliment me for anything, it used to occur to me as their Sarcasm. So many instances I was so willing to go and talk to someone but even before attempting it, I could visualize and think of what worst could happen in that moment and how my proposal shall be rejected badly and I was so good at visualizing it that many times universe manifested it absolutely that way.

When you believe internally that you are not good enough to have a partner and with such a belief even if you get a one, it gives birth to another kind of trait of yours which is Insecurity of losing the person and so you start giving up your Originality and wears the blanket of Pretense of being good so that in every situation the other person remains happy and stick to the relationship because you cannot afford to lose him / her. Such way of being in any relationship never lets the relation flourish as you are not who you are actually. You becomes a person full of fear of losing and trust me people do not want to stay for long with people who are fearful and on mercy of someone. People loves staying with happy people and people who offers space and respect in relationship to them and to himself also. So that one incident changed the way I had relationships in my life.

Most surprising thing which happens with most of us is that we are not even aware of what is happening in our life and why is it happening. We keep searching for root cause on the surface while the actual cause lies deep inside our subconscious and belief system. We work on external factors and gets bothered when nothing changes, it is like typing something wrong on a word file and putting whitener on hard copy or print of document and considering that now the fresh print will have no mistake, but the source document has not been corrected and so every time you will print it, same mistake will be there on printed copy, so in order to have the right print, you have to correct the mistake on source word document. In case of human beings, the source of problem is deep internal ie in our past, our values, thought patterns, beliefs, cultures and it becomes so strong with time that we start living and accepting life that way only till the time we confront that whatever happening in my outside world is nothing but the reflection of my inner world.

Accepting this is not at all easy because the toughest person in this world to work on is - I, myself. It takes a lot to acknowledge that I need to work on myself. Getting new skills is easy but imbibing or accepting new mindset or thought process is toughest of the job.

***

Relationship with my health

That one remark from someone who was family, whom I had respect for, whom my parents had respect for and that one single remark from him changed my whole life upside down. It changed me as a person, it changed my outlook towards me and it changed the way I started seeing myself. And that remark came to me, unfortunately at an age which is considered as one of the most important and critical phase of one's life – adolescent, the teenage – an age when you are about to enter the realms of real world, when you shall be entering the world of real challenges, when you will be facing society and its pressures and challenges and at this time what majorly determines the way you will do and perform in each and everything is how high your Self-esteem is. Self-esteem described as how you see yourself, how you relate you and yourself to success, failures and challenges, what you talk and say to yourself ie what is the quality of your that Inner Voice which is always active inside our head and this inner voice determines our productivity in each and every aspect be it personal, professional, societal, financial or emotional. A high self-esteem almost always ends up having for you a strong and positive Self-Concept and when you move into life carrying a positive self-concept, there are high possibilities of you living a life of happiness, good health, strong relationships and positive accomplishments.

A low self-esteem results in causing lot of mental and physical health issues also because our whole physical body is nothing but the function of our mind and when we live with low self-esteem our brain also struggles in generating the happiness hormones which results in starting of issues like anxiety and depression. Anxiety can also be speech anxiety, people anxiety or task anxiety and it impacts your nervous system as well as your gut health which deteriorates your metabolism and overall health and functioning of every organ in your body.

After that incident, I also gradually started developing one or other issues with my health. Most persistent was digestive issues as my gut health started facing regular issues. As one of the most popular book Heal yourself says that Constipation is nothing but lot of stress accumulated inside along with lack of self-expression and no release of emotions and so was I, whole body filled with complexes and it was showing up through health issues. I lost the grace from my face & there was no glow in my eyes. I started living my life on approval & acceptance of others which was further degrading my confidence and self-esteem.

I developed the body dysmorphic disorder, a mental condition where you keep thinking about one or more defect or flaws in your appearance or looks, a flaw as minor as almost unnoticeable by others, but you always feels embarrassed or so ashamed about it that you starts avoiding any social presence or appearance just in order to avoid any unpleasant encounter which is only and only filmed in your imagination. This disorder really affects your routine & daily actions and your ability to function in routine life as your self-perceived flaw & repetitive behavior starts causing stress to you. BDD makes you focus so intensely on your appearance and you're grooming and looks that every time you are around a mirror, you just keep watching at yourself not with love and compassion but rather with pity and one good look of yours makes you temporarily happy.

I still remember very clearly – my parents lived in Hapur my native town while I started living distant for work and career and whenever I used to go home over the weekends, I just enters home and my first question to my mother or my father used to be "Am I looking weak ?" or "Is my face looking dull?". After few times, my mother started making fun of this (on a lighter note) saying Siddhu (my nick name), maaf karde Hume....

But from my state of mind, asking that question every time was a way of getting an assurance or affirmation from someone that I am not looking bad or I am not looking ugly.

My wife Shikha, we got engaged in June'2013 and we had a courtship period of good 6 months. We used to meet almost every weekend (sometimes during the week also) and just roam around enjoying street foods & chaats, watching movies together as Shikha is a big time fan of King Khan Mr. Shahrukh Khan and no matter if I am willing to watch or not, but going to watch his movie in theatre was an unsaid agreement done between us. She was really understanding as my office calls used to continue till 8 somedays but we decided to not let it ruin our period of love before marriage. My confidence in myself was not really strong and it seemed like Dysmorphic disorder was running in my whole body and I only had complexes and doubts. I still remember, it was 2nd July 2013 and I and Shikha had out first date after our engagement and I was so conscious of what should I wear so that I look good and attractive and it is very natural that when you are so conscious about something, it loses natural flow. I was so doubtful over my appearance, that every time we used to meet, trust me my one common question to Shikha was "Am I looking good? Or Am I looking weak?" And Shikha used to answer me with a very strange look on her face like she is thinking "Why is he even asking this?" and respond "You are looking good Sid" and trust me I never accepted her compliment even then my mind always told me that how can your fiancée criticize your looks on your date so don't take this as compliment but rather her modesty and etiquettes or rather respect towards the relationship.

This amazing behavior of mine continued and re-occurred on our every meeting and finally on our 9th or 10th date, Shikha actually said to me – why you always keep asking this silly question. Sid, you are perfectly fine and you look good. If you will again ask me same question, I am going to call off our engagement, but trust me when she said You Look good – it occurred to me like a consolation to someone who couldn't do well. Very late, I got to know that this is also a syndrome called Imposter Syndrome where in your self-esteem is so low that any acknowledgement given to you for anything lands to you like you don't deserve it and it has come to you by mistake or the accomplishment is just a fluke.

In 2013, just before couple of months of my marriage, my self-esteem was so low because of the pressure of appearing in front of so many people in marriage and my disbelief was so strongly nurtured inside me that I used to think "People will say – such a beautiful girl, she could have got a much better boy" and due to all this and that I developed severe depression & anxiety and lost 6 kgs of weight. My marriage album and photographs will remain as an evidence of this for whole life as I became so skinny at time of my marriage and this added further to my woes. Kept thinking of how will I look at my The Day, my cheeks went inside, glow was missing, skin became rough and there were pimples on face and this whole thing ruined the excitement of that one day which is so special for a person in his or her life and people try their best to look best, to appear best as the memories are stored for ever.

This is what Low Self-esteem is capable of doing to you and your life and this is what one passing remark can do, this is the power of words which can alter your whole life in just one moment and you only keep struggling and keep repairing the patches of your identity crisis. One passing remark can make you the biggest and strongest enemy of yourself and it can make you stand against yourself and barred the growth, happiness, love and harmony from your life.

And why all this happens, because as human beings, we all are nothing but meaning making machines who attach meaning to anything and everything. Be it any situation, any event, any gesture of someone, any words of others or ourselves, whatever happens in that any one moment actually might be attributable to so many other reasons ie why anything happened, why someone responded someway but rather seeing that incident individually we all have this natural immediate reaction of adding some meaning to it like he doesn't likes me, I am not worthy, I don't deserve good, I am unlucky and so on and on and then we starts responding or reacting accordingly. And if you really want to hold a catch of this habit, then just try to be present in the moment and ask yourself before adding any meaning to any event or incident that can I look at this situation from some other empowering perspective? Or am I judging this event rightly? May be other person not meant to insult or embarrass me but rather the person was angry at some other situation or thing that made him reacted that way. And please carry the belief in yourself so that even if some situation is actually against you but you your-self should never ever be.

Here, I invite all my readers who have spent their precious time and hard earned money to buy and read this book, to just go back into your lives and see if ever your words have wounded anyone or any incident or event or if you have been wounded and it changed the course of your life and thoughts. If going through my sharing has opened up something for you and if now you can also realize that it was not that incident actually that shattered you but rather the meaning you created out of that incident or the story your mind created which led you choose the path and made the decisions you made about everything, everyone and you yourself. So here you have this opportunity today to drop all that listening about yourself and start seeing yourself as another wonderful person and give all that love and respect which you always deserved most importantly from yourself. How you can start loving yourself is another wonderful topic of discussion which I will share further in this book.

CHAPTER 4

The Breakthrough

Biggest blessing in life is to have good people around.

In life, any person going through any breakdown cannot normally see himself in the breakdown but other person can. For the person in breakdown, there is something wrong either with himself or his luck or circumstances. Same way, all those 14-15 years, I was never able to or present to the fact that there is no problem with me or my looks or my appearance or my demeanor, rather the problem was with my outlook towards me, the breakdown was with my faith in myself, my love for myself or the way I used to look at myself. There was no problem in fact, it was actually embossed on my mind and my belief by the world around me and then myself, as I never tried to discover – who I am actually but rather told by the people around me and as the confidence and conviction was missing in myself, I bought what they said and made it my identity. This breakdown came into my life at one of the most critical phase of my life as it shook the foundation of me becoming someone extra-ordinary. But every night has a morning and so did my dark night also. It majorly started with my and Shikha's engagement in 2013.

I completed thirty in Feb'2013 and I decided that I should take on the responsibility of finding the girl for myself as I was not really liking now mentioning Marital Status as Single in any kind of document or form (best line I could think or manage to add some humor - lol), so finally I made my profile on one of the popular matrimony portal and start surfing or going through girls profiles, trust me it is quite an interesting thing to do. Just sit down in evenings with a cup of Coffee or tea (as till that time I was not frequently attracted towards beer or scotch) and just keep looking at profiles of so many girls and while you see a profile, you mentally judge whether this girl is Ok for you or your family and toughest question which used to pop up in my mind – will she like my profile? – so it's kind of an on the spot match making happening in your mind and based on that you forward your interest in any profile – hope many of you must have gone through this.

I saw Shikha's profile on the portal and as I bought the paid services of site, I could see her contact details. I took the number mentioned and made the call. I expected the girl to answer the call as its about her life but the voice from other side surprised me that is the age mentioned on profile is correct as the voice doesn't matches but then next moment I got to know that it's her mother's number mentioned on profile, so I shared that I saw your daughter's profile and liked it so wanted to know more and connect and see if we can take things further.

Shikha's mother asked me certain things about myself and my family followed with our parents getting involved into conversations and then the coming Sunday we decided to go and meet Shikha's family, who lives in Ghaziabad. I remember, it was 26th May 2013 when I and my parents along with my sister went to see Shikha and meet her family. I was little nervous, one because of all this arranged marriage meeting setup and second of my own complexes and self-doubts. I was wearing beige color trouser and a check red color shirt and those days I used to have spikes with short hairs.

They lived in a nice colony in a GDA flat on first floor. It was a quite spacious flat with one big living room having kitchen on one side, one small room just opposite to entry wall and another room or kind of temporary enclosure, and then two bedrooms with one common washroom in between. Our hometown house also has good space but as being a very old setup, it is not that planned like a flat has.

We entered the house and I saw Shikha, her big eyes is surely the first things anyone shall notice on her face and it makes her look attractive (even today). Families started talking to each other while we were served tea and some snacks. Tea made by Shikha's father, which I came to know after marriage only, was always done by Papa only at their house. As expected, parent asked us both to go and talk separately if we wish, to which I was little hesitant as it was a homely setup and I was little uncomfortable to talk private at a girl's house at very first meeting though I wanted to as we were meeting for a very critical and important decision of our life, but before I could say anything, thankfully Shikha said yes to this and asked me to go and sit in another room and have a chat. Fortunately, both families found everything okay and we decided to stay together for rest of life, thus very next Sunday, I and Shikha got engaged and from here started my journey of rising back and knowing the actual Siddharth which was buried under so the burden of that one remark made on me 15 years back and this journey of my peeling out one by one the layers of my complexes and inhibitions gave myself a new life and whatever I am today is only because of few wonderful and beautiful souls God has sent into my life.

Officially from 3rd June 2013, I and Shikha had our 6 months of courtship period and I was always nervous and super-conscious of my appearance and looks whenever I had to meet Shikha. After couple of casual conversations and dates, as we both started getting opened up to each other, every time we used to meet, I used to ask her if I am looking good and every time her Yes was with the tone of like thinking in her head – "Why he asks this every time?" and trust me when she did compliment me, my imposter syndrome used to become active immediately and tell me, she is just being courteous – do not take it seriously. At one of date, we went to one of the Mall in Noida and were having food, when Shikha asked me specifically – Why you are always asking the same question? do you think, you don't look good. Though answering this was so easy for me but I could not answer her that day and just said… Nothing like that, it's just that I am little gallant kind of person, but I could sense that day that Shikha has smelled my low self-esteem and disbelief in myself and my appearance.

And this happens when you have beautiful souls in your life, Shikha started acknowledging my looks and appearance from then, though initially my mind did not accept it and kept repeating to myself "that's not true", but continuous recurrence started slowly changing me internally. She used to compliment me over my height, my overall demeanor, the way I eat, the way I talk and I actually understood very late what actually she was doing to me. She tried her best to make me believe that I do not lack anything, that I am complete, whole and perfect. She also tried to assure me that my looks and appearance has no relevance in our relationship, only my true being, my character has and what I am from inside.

Shikha gradually succeed in having me understand that it's not the lack or absence of anything rather the confidence, self-love and belief in myself which is missing and because of this I was always so keen to do things which I think can help me to overcome these issues and as Shikha was already part of an education which helps people meet their real potential and complete with their past, bad relationships, failures or believe that every human being has ability to become extra-ordinary. The group or education have their own set of specific and unique techniques which they ask you to go through during respective sessions and if you are ready to undergo that discomfort and the confrontation to your already set identity, they make available a whole new world opened up for you and change the way you see yourself, your life and each and every aspect around. They make you present to fact that it's not just others but you also have a listening of yourself and if you can alter that, you can alter everything because you're listening in your own world makes you do whatever you do and makes you think whatever you think. Shikha told me about this education one day and I got sold to that immediately and this was the beginning of another Chapter of my transformation.

We got engaged in June'14 and I got myself registered in that education in July'14, the initial level course which was of 3 days 9 AM to 10 PM ie Friday, Saturday and Sunday. At first, when I got to know about the schedule, I was little scared as who shall sit for such a long time and that too in a class but trust me except for first day first half, remaining two and half days were like super amazing and super evolving.

I entered the Centre (place where 3 days session was scheduled / planned), it was a standalone two storied building with one basement & an open space in front for 6-8 car parking, a reception cum office area on ground floor, and a side entry which takes you to Seminar hall in basement and rear side staircase. On entrance gate, I found a guy and a lady both neatly dressed in formals and wearing their name tags, they both were there with a bright smile and wished me Good Morning and I was like- "Do I know them?", anyways I proceeded to the floor where the session was scheduled. It was a big hall with well-polished wooden doors, floor built of high quality lustrous marble with green granite square boundaries, and the room had windows on all three side of with lacquered polish wooden frames and glass work. There was a small stage and two mikes fixed on stands one on each side of stage. I was little petrified as there were more than 200 chairs arranged in the room and seeing them I thought, is this really going to be that big group and if yes, then will I be able to participate or talk or answer anything. Hope they will not call me on stage to share anything and trust me the thought itself gave me an anxiety feeling. Sharp at 9 AM, a gentleman entered the room and took the stage area. He was clean shaved having worn spectacles, wearing well ironed white formal shirt with metal shanks and royal blue pants, shirt was tucked in so nicely that the centre of shirt and belt was exactly aligned. He carried such a bright and vibrant smile on his face that just seeing his confidence, I started thinking and praying to God to please make me as good and as confident as him – no fear, no inhibition – just being there fully. His aura was charismatic.

In those three days, I realized that I am not the only one who is suffering from this fatal disease called Low confidence and self-esteem and also that there are bigger problems in people's lives. I saw people going in front and sharing their problems, I saw people asked by Coach to come on stage and share what that person felt of the last conversation or distinction created, I saw people resisting to go on mic, trembling, stammering but the Coach and other participants also provided people the space and listening and allowed even the most scared people to open up and speak and this gave me also the courage to raise my hand during one of the sessions which was on relationships and the baggage we carry on ourselves and that was the day I spoke first time ever in my life in front of more than two hundred people rather two hundred strangers though initially I was not able to speak properly but no idea what religious space that session, leader and other participants provided me, I opened up a little.

It was the day, I transformed and caused my relationship with my younger brother – Paritosh and also to some extent with my own self also. I always dreamt of having a real friend like relationship with my brother but something stopped me always from being a friend of him. That day, during one of the session, while one guy was sharing something from his life, I was stupefied, I was numbed as for me it was not that person sharing his life but rather like he has read some chapters from my life and just narrating it with some alterations or amendments. I was even little bewildered as to how can two people have so similar stories of their lives which I later realized that when source is similar the issues are also somehow similar and the source was NO Self-love and low self-esteem. When he shared what happened in his life and Coach started working with him, I could clearly see what was missing in the relationship of me and my brother and it was all missing from my end only, trust me my younger brother was more than being a brother to me always but I had filters on my eyes and so was never able to see his love and respect for myself. For me, it was like I was standing there on stage and sharing my life and now Coach is working with me to confront and cause what matters to me but there was still something missing and it was to confront it openly and take the responsibility of my actions in past and take on responsibility of transforming this relationship of me and my brother.

When Coach concluded with that guy and asked everyone if anyone wants to ask anything or share anything that opened up from that last sharing and conversation, it was first time in my life I felt that way. My mind, my heart and my body were in so much conflict to each other as I wanted to take this opportunity and raise my hand to go in front and share what I got out of the conversation but that anxiety, that fear of being public and being exposed to that possibility of being embarrassed again, it was putting so much weight on my hand and shoulder muscles that my arm was almost numb and frozen. In that moment, there were multiple Siddharth in me, one saying go and take this opportunity, other one saying DO NOT - don't you remember what can happen if you go public, another one saying go and kill your fear as it can be that one last opportunity to cause your relationship with your brother. And this is the beauty of this Cosmic Power and this Universe that when you are really looking to cause something, it aligns all energies in support of you and that's when I had an eye contact with FL and don't know how but he gauged that a sharing is about to explode out of my mouth and body and it was the moment when I heard FL saying "Yes Sid, please come as I can see - you really want to share something". I never experienced such an amazing mix of feelings where I am happy as well scared and petrified, my legs were shaking and there were butterflies in my tummy. I was wearing a green T-shirt with black jeans and beige loafers with my hairs neatly spiked with gel and clean shaved and I finally went and grabbed the mic and when I raised my eyes to the room, I had another wave of anxiety seeing so many people sitting there in room and all looking at me but then again FL broke the silence and asked me "Sid, so tell me what do you do, where you work, where you come from" and then he asked everyone to give a big hand to me and acknowledge the courage it needs to come up and share anything from your life and thank God that nice applause from everyone comforted me a bit. I was still very nervous and anxious, it's been 15 years of that incident but that experience was still so present there in my mind and body, it was like it has happened recently with me.

'Good morning everyone' – I spoke and greeted everyone to which everyone responded with energy and warmness which actually filled the room with different energy.

I started my sharing first acknowledging the person who's sharing opened up this for me, still remember his name – Tejasvi.

"While Tejasvi was sharing from his life, I was shocked as to me how can we have so similar areas of struggle but thanks Tejasvi, because had you not shared here today, don't know if I would have gathered courage to share what

I am going to share now" – I said with a warm thanking voice.

"It is about my relationship with my younger brother named Paritosh, who is seven years younger to me. Though I have always been a very sincere and responsible child in my family, but there has been a different Siddharth altogether residing inside me when it comes about me and my brother's relationship. Since last so many years, I wanted both of us to be two good friends who can just be frank and honest to each other, can talk and discuss anything and trust me, he was always available but I was never there and not there because I was carrying so many complaints and incompletions with him while he never gave me any opportunity to have any complaint because he is a wonderful brother but it was all from my end only"

My voice started getting heavier as was my heart.

"I always carried this complex of not being good with my looks and appearance like all other family members of mine and this feeling of being deprived took away from me the love for my own self. Paritosh was really so good looking and lovable and he was born talent as he can play any musical instrument and as he kept recceiving love and admiration, I kept getting more and more envy and jealous of him and more insecure with everyday passing and without he being aware of any of this developing inside me, he always respected me and loved me".

Continued with my tears almost out of my eyes.......

"I only started finding ways to criticize him and many a times I did beat him also just to make sure that he gets defamed inside the family and do not gets love what he has been getting always".

"In last few years, when I started understanding that what I am doing is not right and intensity of my envy also started getting lower, I then wanted to fill this void between us, I wanted to change and be with him like I wished to be but that past baggage of my acts and thoughts and my behavior towards him did not allow me to move ahead and take a step towards re-creating and causing the beautiful relationship of two brothers. I was not able to find the access and even today, this stands as a blind spot for me, an area which I want to transform but have no idea – HOW?"

There was silence in the room for about 10-15 secs as I was almost in tears and also felt like being naked there in front of so many people but to transform, I think you need to be courageous and face the shit.

FL's voice broke the silence suddenly when he asked me.

"Sid, how much you want to get your brother back?"

"Do you want to transform this relationship with your brother today?"

"Are you ready to take on this, trust me, this can be tough, very confronting, very uncomfortable but really worth it"

"Yes Coach" – I said.

"Then just call him and whatever you shared to us here, say to him" – FL said.

"I know, it really takes a lot to say Sorry to your younger brother and especially when you have always been a responsible child in your family, but trust me Sid, that's the only way to bring back the love and your lost relationship with your brother" – FL continued

"And do not just say sorry to him, also create with him or share to him that from here what kind of relationship you want to have with him, so what's your vision of this relationship. Sid, we have never been told by anyone in our life the power of Acknowledgement. When you acknowledge something, you have the power on your side to re-create it and that's what you will experience when you will acknowledge - who you were with him, how it impacted this relationship and what you want to be now"

"You do not need to do anything big, just go and say sorry to him for everything you did to him and for every feeling you carried for him and also tell him why you behaved that way for so long, tell him that you always felt that he is much better in looks than you and that's the reason he used to get all the love, at-least that's how it used to occur to you. I invite you to drop all your ego and be there hundred percent in that moment, taking responsibility of your each and every action towards him and allow yourself to complete the past and create a future which empowers you to live your life with your brother the way you have been wanting.

Just do it and experience & see the magic of Power of Creation, and when you will be back in session tomorrow, we will have your Sharing which might inspire someone sitting here having similar challenge in his or her life, in one or other relationship but not able to gather courage and come up and share, so Sid here I take this opportunity to acknowledge you and your courage to come up and share your Inauthenticity with your brother and allow all of us also to see again the reaffirmation of this powerful saying – "When you confront, you get access to Transformation".

The moment was so magical and the energy in room was so pure that I felt like hugging the leader but their protocols did not allow me to do so. In that one single moment, when FL just completed what he wanted to conclude with, I had so many thoughts going in my head as I was less of words to thank Shikha as she provided me access to such a wonderful place where you are provided a listening with no judgement, something which is not so commonly available in world outside. While I was just trying to be normal and take hold of myself, I heard a loud applause all around the room, all participants were clapping like anything and it was THE moment for me. I went back to my seat with tears in my eyes and my next seated participant (Madhur) stood up and gave me a tight hug. I took my seat with a very light weighed heart as I could feel that burden removed from my soul, the burden, the baggage and load of my smallness and inauthenticity, of all those years of splurge where I was pretending to be honest and responsible in my relationship with my younger brother but I was actually someone else.

It was first time in my life, when I talked and connected with so many new people, whom I have never met and I could feel my age old fear of people dissipating a bit.

But the real task was yet to be completed ie calling my younger brother and saying sorry to him. Honestly, sharing my inauthenticity in front of so many people was easy but shredding down your identity in front of someone who has always seen you as a responsible brother and telling him that all these years, I was jealous of you and hated you at so many instances, was carrying complex with you as you were always good looking while I was not – this is something big to do. My sharing ended on that day around 3 in afternoon and FL asked me to complete with my brother after that session only or latest by tonight else the possibility of being a real brother with him might fade, but even at the end of the day, I could not gather courage to call my brother. I left from the venue at around 9:30 and reached home around 10:15 PM and every second, every minute there was a battle inside between two identities of myself – one saying leave it, just be normal with him and all the lost love and affinity will resume itself in sometime, while the other Siddharth saying – jus break this barrier today Sid, pick the phone and complete with him because your brother deserves a sorry for what all feelings and incompletions you had with him and whatever impact he has borne due to that. It is the time for you to confront your inauthenticity and transform this relationship in a moment. My phone became so heavy during this whole conversation of me and my soul, that I was not able to pick it up and make the call, but as time was passing and I promised the FL that I will do this today only, I finally just picked up the phone and dialed his number. Trust me, while it was ringing, I was praying to God in my mind that I wish he doesn't pick the call, as then I can escape saying that I tried but he didn't pick the phone, but when you tries to resist something, its occurrence speeds up and so Paritosh picked up the call.

"Hello Siddhu bhaiya" – I could hear his sound from other side as that's how he always addresses me, even today.

"Hello Ghaniya" – I replied

I continued saying – "What's going on ?, kya kar raha hai" and while he answered to this but I was so anxious and nervous that I was not listening to him and only preparing in my mind – what and how to say and where to begin from...

There was ocean of thoughts and emotions running through the body, there was this fear of losing my respect by sharing my inauthenticity to him, an insecurity of losing my credibility of being a responsible brother and son, but then I was on the edge of confronting my fear and creating another possibility of love and oneness with my brother and this possibility made me speak ...

"Wanted to talk to you about something, free hai abhi, baat kar sakte hai ?" - I said

"What happened bhaiya, all well?" - he said

Wanted to discuss is a very scary line and especially when you say this to someone close, their first instinct is always an emotion of worry and I could feel the same emotion in his voice over the phone.

"Bhai, I wanted to say sorry to you for every single thing I did to you which I should not have. You have been such an amazing and wonderful brother always, but it was I, who was jealous of you because of my insecurity and my complexes with my looks and appearance" - I said

"How many drinks down today" - he asked, as in 23 years of our relationship, we never spoke like this and for him, it was certainly not a small thing, I saying sorry to him.

"Nah bhai, I am in complete senses but now I cannot carry this inauthenticity anymore, I want us to live life like two brothers who are there for each other always and in every situation, who are just not brothers but two good friends, who can discuss anything be it money, family, girls, beer, sex - anything"

"I always used to feel that everybody loves you more because you are so good looking and also a born talent* and I am not loved that much and this atrocious thought process of mine took me into a whole world of my inhibitions and complexes and made me feel deprived always and all this made me a different person altogether".

*(Paritosh has this gift of god that he can play any instrument without any coaching or training).

I continued – "I don't know when I walked away so far from this relationship of ours, always feeling deprived and unabundant, always trying and finding avenues to criticize you as for me that was the only way to make you look small in eyes of others and to get for myself the love and attention".

"I would like to say sorry for every damn thing I did and from here now, I am taking the responsibility of becoming a real actual brother to you, someone with whom you can talk and share anything and everything."

I paused and that's when he said "nah bhaiya, don't say like this and let bygones be bygones, for me you have always been a person I look upto and trust me bhaiya .. aap bahut ache lagte ho. Even my friends appreciates you and your personality. Take care of yourself and have a good sleep now".

"Ok bhai, take care, good night" – I replied. Though it was tough to say as never said that, but I closed the call saying "Love you bhai". This is so ironical that we hesitate saying these three golden words to the people in our lives whom we love the most and without whom our world is not complete.

I invite every reader that just take out time and go to person you love and tell that person that you love them, just say "I Love you and thanks for being there in my life and making it so beautiful" and I know that they are aware of your love for them, but love is an emotion which enhances and expands when we say it and acknowledges the importance of other person, doing it from your heart and authentically. Sometimes words are required to let the other person know what you feel for them and how important they are for you and when we do it honestly and share from our heart, it reaches other person's heart as it is never two people that communicates, it is always two sub-conscious minds talking to each other and what we have inside reaches the other person's sub-conscious through our vibes, our thoughts, our emotions and our eyes.

We all have heard so many times in our life that transformation of anything starts always with being uncomfortable but I actually experienced it first ever time in my life personally as since the morning when I shared it during session and when I was asked by Coach to call my brother and complete this today, I was very uncomfortable inside as there was a continuous debate inside me between my identity and the new possibility. Making call to Paritosh was not easy and I dragged doing it till the last minute wishing I do not have to do this today and will make an excuse tomorrow in session but trust me all this getting uncomfortable, uneasy, getting in confrontation with my own being was more than worth it as after having that conversation with him, I felt so good inside, so light on my soul and suddenly something magical happened to me which was a rise in my love for myself which has been missing inside me for ages and that's when I experienced first time in my life personally that doing something out of your comfort zone, something which challenges your identity to cause something new gives an adrenaline rush to your self-love and self-esteem because it breaks somewhere your perception about your own self that you cannot do it and when it breaks, it opens up a new listening of yourself in your own world – a powerful listening.

That night, an aspect of my life transformed forever and it did not happen just in the relationship with my brother but on many other places also, as a slight shift in your being creates an impact on so many areas of your life and it all happened because of just one action taken my me ie Made a call to him and we all have people in our lives without whom we are incomplete but yet due to one or other small reason or argument or debate or misunderstanding we have given up on that relationship and have allowed our ego ruin the love and affinity of that relationship, so here is your assignment – just go back to your life and see if there's any such relationship which can be recreated or regenerated by just a simple sorry for whatever you have done or have been into that relationship, get present to your inauthenticity into that relationship and talk to that person from your heart and let the warmness of this possibility of recreation of the relationship reach other person's heart through your words and emotions and trust me you will see that even other person was so eagerly willing to have that love back into that relationship but it was just EGO from both sides which was stopping both to come together again and cause it back.

This can be your relationship with your parents, your siblings, any friend or any other person – I invite you to be cause in the matter which means you move ahead and take the responsibility of bringing back the love into that relationship.

So many people in this world have incompletions with their parents and many of them have given up even talking to their mother or father or both and you will find majority of them struggling in their own lives in one or more major aspects. Having all the money, luxury cars, big homes but they find a void space inside and that peace missing in life and they could rarely understand the reason which is actually their bad relationship with their parents. Please understand, we all human beings are like tree and like a tree cannot grow strong and tall with weak roots, we also cannot attain complete success with having an unhealthy relationship with our parents as they are our source on this planet and anything not connected to his / her / its source in life will always struggle in becoming whole, perfect and complete. So if you are one of those who have major issues in your relationship with your parents, no matter if it was them who were at fault, no matter if they have been unfair to you, just forgive them and be grateful for everything they did right to you and tell them whatsoever – you love them. Just doing this will detoxify your mental space, it will boost your love for yourself and you will experience a different peace at your soul. We all leave examples for our kids through our actions and forgiving your parents will also show your kids that elders can also be wrong at times but they still deserve love, respect and forgiveness.

***

Next morning, it was like a different world for me and I was so excited to go to the second day of session and share with everyone what I have caused last night. It was Saturday morning and I entered the Centre with a very different confidence and excitement today, we all reached the classroom as being Punctual is a significant part of Integrity there. That space had some sacred energy flowing always as just being there you feel like you are into some other world where you can share anything and your sharing, your truth will be heard and preserved with utmost dignity and respect and without any judgement and this space made so many people opened up and share from their lives what we can't just think of sharing to anyone in outside world and that too when you are all strangers to each other.

If there is one thing which is really missing in world outside is unfiltered listening, a listening where you are not judged, you are not given any advises but you are just allowed to speak and empty yourself and allow yourself to focus on something more relevant and important and start afresh from the point of Nothing and that's why Social Media has become so significant part of our lives as it just do not stops you from sharing whatever you feel like doing and never judges you back.

"Who would like to share what you caused out of yesterday's session or assignment?" - When FL asked during the session, I immediately raised my hand and raised it really high so that I should not get overlooked.

And on third turn, I got opportunity to go up on mic and share what I accomplished. I shared everything about how I tried to delay it, how we talked and what was my experience sharing my inauthenticity and completing it with Paritosh and that's when FL patted on my back and asked everyone to give a round of applause for the courage shown by me to do and cause it. And then FL shared something which gave me a new insight about life and the purpose behind taking sharing of people who have caused anything out of the assignment of first day of session.

FL speaking – "The purpose of taking sharing is that when a person comes up here and shares what he / she has accomplished, it opens up so many things for the people listening to the sharing and actually people sitting there and listening to sharing do not actually only listens but also starts peeping into their own lives and tell themselves that I can also do this and cause something worthy in my life, because when someone shares, there are many others sitting in room dealing with almost same kind of issues but lot of them dealing with lack of confidence & courage which doesn't allows them to rise and speak in front of so many people, so you sharing from here is not actually just you sharing alone but rather sharing as a representative of a group of people having similar concerns and for this I thank you Siddharth for allowing transformation reach to so many people in this classroom".

"Also, when you are sharing what you have accomplished, in front of so many people, it turns your accomplishment into a declaration that this was not just a one day thing but from here now I have taken on the responsibility of being a real responsible and lovable brother to Paritosh and you can be held accountable by anyone here for deviating from your word and this is the Power of Declaration." – He continued.

Now, not all of you are going to attend a class room session of so many people to declare something in your lives, but you can also use the Power of Declaration by just sharing to people around you what you want to create or cause. So for example, if you want to write a book and it is only you who knows about your this wish then the chances are high that this may get fade with time and struggles and other priorities of life, but just imagine that you have already told your family, your friends , your colleagues that I am starting to write a book and will have it published in one year's time then you might even forget it at times but the people around you will keep reminding you just by asking that what is the progress on your book, some might even make fun of it but all this will keep you present to the declaration made by you that You promised to write a book and chances are high that just to avoid having your listening as an ostentatious person, you shall start writing the book.

Another example: if you want to lose weight, then just take a pic of yours and post it on FB, Insta or on your WhatsApp DP and declare that I will lose 10 kgs in next 3 months and rest will be taken care of by the people around you ie they will not allow you to forget your declaration.

Let me tell you – this is the outcome of Power of Declaration only that I am writing this book, because I shared it to so many people and after that whenever we used to meet or talk, they always used to ask me "What about your book". Some of my friends even said to me "bhai likh bh raha hai ya bas aise hi", so finally I started, so thanks to all those who held me accountable for my declaration.

Those three days session changed a lot inside me, it gave a new hope of confidence and self-belief to me and especially after my sharing, as people came to me during breaks and appreciated what I did. Centre had a space on their third floor of building, a covered space which, as told by one of the centre staff, is also used to conduct sessions in case there is space crunch for any session. During the forums, centre used that floor as Cafeteria and they used to call a vendor named Brown Sugar who provided a make shift arrangement for people to have lunch and used to serve food combos like Rice & Rajma/Choley/Dal etc along with some snacks like sandwiches, momos and I specially loved their wheat momos, though by that time, I had never been really fond of momos but this session not here not only changed my perception about myself but also about momos and I started liking it.

I still remember, it was second day during lunch break, I took a plate of wheat momos and a sandwich and I was enjoying my lunch with couple of session mates standing round on a high table, when three ladies came to our table and said.

"Hi Sid" - one of them said. She must be in her late forties, very elegantly dressed up in Cotton saree, hairs half locked.

"Hello ma'am" - I said

"You were amazing at your sharing, both yesterday and today morning. What you have accomplished is not easy to do. And I am surprised, that you think you do not look good, you look so handsome Sid" - She said.

And then what she said next - gave me a new perspective.

"Sid, take my words, till the time, you yourself don't starts believing in you, keep borrowing the other's belief in you, because many times in life, its others who can see what you are capable of, more than you do. Trust me, you are an amazing person" - she said this to me and said thanks and bye and left for the session, but what she said to me before leaving left me stunned and thinking that I don't know what extraordinary has she seen in me that made her acknowledge me so powerfully as I have the Imposter syndrome still residing in me.

Appreciations & all these acknowledgements really uplifted my confidence and esteem and this three day training helped my self-love sprout out of the surface a little bit, which was buried deep 14-15 years ago by that one incident. Heard it times before that the power of acknowledgement is very strong and it can open up people towards each other and helps them connect better but felt it first time personally in life as all these acknowledgements had somehow managed to have me a connect with my own being and with the person staying inside me and it paved the way for the beginning of my personal transformation.

CHAPTER 5

The Rise

The Power of Association

Some wonderful man once said 'A man only learns in two ways – either by reading or by association with smarter people'.

Early in my life, I realized that to achieve anything significant, I will have to work hard and find better ways to accomplish my dreams, though initially and for a very long time, I had no clue what I should do or pursue to be successful. I did things but found that those were not aligned with my destination of dreams and so I always kept looking for some or the other proposals wherein I could grow both in terms of my finances and also overcome my fear of people, especially when it comes to talking to those people who are better than me in terms of money, authority and appearance. And yes I always wanted to make lots of money in my life because I wanted to experience how it feels when there is no conversation of money in your life & how your outlook towards people and life alters. Majority of working population on this planet works only for money but not to pursue their passion. Majority of people are only doing what life throws at them and they could not find other ways to earn a living & take care of themselves and dependants and so the choice has been missing.

As mentioned in Ikigai, if your purpose in life is clear, it keeps you disciplined, focused and motivated. It gives you reason every morning to jump out of your bed, irrespective of whether it's a good or bad day. It gives you enough energy to stay on track. When you have a clear purpose you feel complete and finds serenity even if surrounded by world of restlessness because you clearly knows what needs to be done. It is always the lack of clarity or the state of ambiguity that causes anxiety or stress. And so having a clear purpose keeps you mentally healthy which in place keeps you healthy physically as body is a function of the mind.

Out of my search for something, I associated with a Direct Selling company in 2016. I started as an Affiliate with one of the reputed companies which decided to use Network Marketing as a way to distribute and sell their products. I will not be promoting any specific business or industry or concept here, but today I personally believe that every young male or female who has just completed his / her college education should work once into an Affiliate Marketing or Network Marketing. This is not just to make money but more importantly to learn the most critical traits and lessons of practical life which neither school education nor any professional education ever gives us. No body teaches us in school or college about how to deal with people, how to talk to people, how to handle rejections and failures, how to maintain perseverance and patience in business and in life as well, how to rise back after a breakdown. Can you imagine the life of a person who has been taught all this right from school times and given people and public skills trainings during college days? I am sure that the personality of such person at time of graduating from school or college will be exemplary & his or her attitude towards people, life or work will be top-notch. I am sure that this attitude and mindset earned so early in life will make them understand the most basic thing of life that without managing people well and without managing your emotions during tough times, you cannot achieve anything big in life.

When I started working on business, I was not very confident as Network Marketing is all about talking to people, showing them the business, handling their objections and closing the Sale and then making your team learn the whole process. Unlike corporate job, in affiliate marketing you have people in your team who are way smarter than you and people who have already achieved a lot in life, people who are already in their own business other than this, but as they were also open to look for something else where they can grow the way they wanted their other business to grow and develop a strong passive income, so they comes to affiliate marketing. The possibility of building a system and a passive income is legitimately available in this industry considering you do it with sheer sincerity and integrity.

Now having such people in your team who have more experiences of life and business than you and you have to lead the team, can you imagine what kind of work you will have to do on yourself, what kind of learnings you need to grab and what kind of confidence it needs for you to overcome your self-doubts and believe in yourself and your ability that you can do it and yes there is no doubt about it that when you work, talk, sit, eat and party with people smarter than you, you become more smart and more experienced in almost every aspect of your character and personality as there is something called The Rubbing Effect which says that you become the average of five people you spent most of your time with and during that whole 3-4 years of duration, I spent lot of time with so many good people that I learned so much from them and the most beautiful thing which happened to me and which actually transformed the person inside me was that my team mates, my mentors, they all believed in me and my success and my ability way more than I did.

As the saying goes "Keep telling the person that he is wonderful, until he starts believing it" and that's what they did to me as well. As their belief and trust in me was constant, it gradually started making me also believe that I can also do something and I am no exception for having success in my life, it's just that I have to first start believing that I deserve success and I can get it and then just start doing whatever it takes to reach there, be it learning from someone who is doing better than me, taking trainings, reading books, being in the association of right people, breaking my own boundaries and boundaries as small as like controlling my home sickness, controlling my habit of leaving early from trainings or dropping a session for just being at home on weekends and spending time with family.

Trust me, when you make even a small alteration to what your mind tells you to do, this little confrontation makes a big impact to your identity. Such small steps starts giving message to your being that you are capable of controlling your mind, your inner voice and it gives your self-esteem and self-love a big push. I was introduced to affirmations, power of gratitude and your words, during that journey only and I started practicing all this. That journey of 3-4 years made me a strong person in terms of facing failures and rejections and still keep standing tall and all this changed my thought process, mindset and my attitude.

One big fear during those times when I was working actively as an affiliate was meeting a completely new person, a stranger and having to explain the whole business model. I was even Ok explaining the numbers as I a little analytical in my approach and making someone understand the numbers was in the bucket of my strong suit. But before you show the numbers or talk about business, you should know the person, understand what he is there for and is he really looking for something or is just here to meet. This was sort of like ice-breaking before presenting the business and this was something I was really not comfortable doing and I silently used to pray and hope that I wouldn't be asked to do it. But then any transformation is always uncomfortable, so one day was asked suddenly by my mentor to go and meet a businessman who has been invited by one of our team mate for business discussion. I asked my mentor to please ask someone else to do it as I was not at all prepared. What he told me next changed something inside me and I still carry it with me today. He said – Sid, that person who is sitting inside does not know what is to be discussed, the right or wrong about the model or the business or anything. He will only believe what you will share with full conviction and belief, he will not listen to what you will say but what you believe inside. He can see it in your eyes if you are saying something just for the sake of saying or if you actually mean it. So I invite you here that before going into the meeting, ask yourself first that

Do I really believe in what I am doing?

Do I have the intent of really making him a partner or I am just looking to make a sale?

Do I really believe that this business can make a difference in his life and if I fail to make him part of it today, it's not us but rather him who will be at loss?

Do I believe in our product and the opportunity?

So Sid, give yourself five minutes of silence and self-talk and ask yourself these questions and if the answer is not satisfactory then I will ask someone else to take this meeting.

That one conversation with my mentor that day transformed the way I looked at Sales and Business from that very moment. I entered the meeting with full confidence, yes I was still nervous but that nervousness was not stopping me from taking the action and doing what had been assigned to me.

We all experience this in one or other area of our lives, when we are really doubtful or anxious about doing something, we feel nervous, our feet freezes, our mind clogs and we feel lost. But then ask yourself that if whatever you are supposed to do, is going to make a difference in the life of your client, your family, your kids, your parents or anyone who will be impacted by your actions and then just take a deep breath and play your role in that specific moment be it any business meeting or training or session and you will see the difference in outcome yourself.

Success is not always measured in terms of money or financial gains, as I could not make the amount of money I thought I will from the business but I made way more than that in terms of what kind of person I became in those 3-4 years of my association with the project. It made me start believing in myself, I became an avid reader and till today I keep reading one or other book, be it any motivational book, be it about patriotism, country's independence, biography of any successful person as every book teaches you something and makes you a better person. Whatever I am today as a person has a huge contribution of that journey and as someone said- "It's not what you get, it's what you become out of a journey that makes the real difference".

And during that journey only, when I conceived my dream of writing a book which I am living today.

So, all my dear readers, be with the right people as the power of association can do wonders in your life, leave your homes, leave your couches, leave your phones and all that hours of time we all waste surfing social media, go to clubs, parks, attend seminars, trainings, try to connect with people who are doing better than you, start reading books – trust me even the most successful people on this planet reads and reads and reads because books connect you to the world. Start what you have been thinking of ages but never initiated because the fear of failure, the fear of uncertainty has hold your feet tight but the pain of failure is always less than the guilt of not attempting in life, even if you fail you will become better at something and from there when you will attempt again, the chances will be high that you will make it and if unfortunately you fail again then just

TRY IT AGAIN ....

Like a kid who doesn't stops when he falls, he just goes on trying and trying and finally celebrates the victory.

And please do watch out what you say to yourself and what you talk to yourself as it will have the maximum impact on whatever you do in life and whatever you will accomplish – be the first one in this whole world to accept, love and embrace yourself and you will see the world in coherence with you and your beliefs.

Now we all have heard a lot about loving yourself, be in love with you or so, but like everything in this world, loving yourself can be learned as it is a process which if learned and followed can make you a different person altogether. Just by accepting the fact that I need to love myself might not give you access to it until unless we know what and how we need to do to be in love with our own self.

So, let's talk in detail about how we can practice and generate love and respect for our self, in the next and last chapter of this book.

CHAPTER 6

How to love yourself

Why is this even a question? Do we ever ask how to eat food, how to breath air – No, right? But then how to love yourself has become so relevant topic because of the conditioning of us in world.

Is loving yourself bad or is it being selfish or self-centered putting yourself first or is it right people won't like you much if you think about yourself first? A certain answer might be YES (though it is actually not true), but that's how we all have been taught or told by our parents, family, school or society. As a kid, we all listen to this so many times, that always think about others, people who only thinks about themselves are not loved by others. We all must have seen, if any kid or teenager spending time on himself or herself, family starts telling them things like – always thinking about yourself or you should not so focused on yourself. Now, trust me, nowhere am I saying that we should not think of others, we have been given this life as a human being to serve people and humanity, spread love and affinity on planet, be compassionate for others, carry love and care for others, as that's the only proven way to make this world an amazing place to live and cherish, but an ironical fact is that no human being can be in-service to others without being in-service to himself first, no person on this planet can spread or offer love without having love in his heart for himself. Love is like money in your account, to lend it to someone else, you must first have it in your own account or else even if you are willing to help someone with it, you cannot as your own bank account is NIL. So what happens, when we as kid hears all those teachings or conversations in family or around us, this conditioning silently starts getting infused into our sub-conscious, that thinking to love yourself or putting yourself on priority or be a little selfish is not considered good among people or in society and then even if someone do this checks doubly as the person remains bothered of him being considered as Self-centered or not so good human being. Person feels guilty because their thoughts or actions are not in alignment what they have been taught and what we all have been hearing from your parents and have accepted it as our values, so doing anything in contrast to that makes you feel bad and from there starts the string of self-beating, blaming & self-cursing.

It's not that our parents or family aimed to teach us wrong, NO, but we were not told the full truth and the full truth is that we should love all the people around, the only change is that you should be the first person in that list.

Let me ask you something, can you make someone learn driving if you yourself doesn't know how to drive? can you be a good teacher, without being a good student yourself first?, can you help someone physically without being healthy yourself first?, can you show the right path to someone without being on right path yourself? Can you help someone with money, being a bankrupt yourself?, I hope you must have answered the same response to all above questions and ie NO, then how can you love anyone else without loving yourself first, I read a beautiful slogan somewhere and it goes like "Raise yourself to help mankind" – trust me, only those have the power of transforming this world who have first raised themselves – No education, No affinity, No compassion, No love, No sprit of serving others simply means No Transformation and to have all this for others have it for yourself first and then only you might be able to offer it to the World.

Now there has always been so many discussions around loving yourself, but irony is that knowing doesn't makes a difference alone, until unless you make knowledge marry the actions and for actions we all need a path, process or plan which we can follow and achieve the desired outcome. So, here I am listing out things or practices we can start doing immediately if not all at once but picking some of them but what matters is doing them consistently and with lot of self-discipline, yes it is the key word to have self-love. I cannot assure your success but I can surely guarantee your failure if the practices are not followed with discipline and then this will be just another book or content you would have gone through on context of How to love yourself.

Here are some very easy yet so powerful practices which we can start following and reap the benefits.

Be kind to yourself

We all have this habit of victimizing, criticizing, beating and blaming our self for anything and everything that doesn't goes well or as per our expectation. An average human being speaks or talks around 60 minutes a day, as a study suggests, but actually we keep talking every moment till we are awake and most of the talking we do is with our own self and unfortunately most of that self-talk is mostly not healthy ie either we are compressing our self or cursing our self or comparing our self on one or other thing. Trust me, the most important talk is the talk you do with yourself and it determines how well you do in anything you attempt. No matter if the whole world is out there to curse or blame you but there is one person who should never be doing that and that is YOU. Its Ok to be into problems, making mistakes, taking wrong decisions but no matter what circumstances you are into, always be respectful, loving and caring towards yourself as this gives you lot of love for yourself.

Stop comparing & start acting

With social media taking over so much space into our lives, it has become so easy to get influenced by others and then start feeling deprived or start comparing yourself to others. Never ever never do that, never compare yourself with others, it degrades your self-dignity and esteem which dents your self-love. Every human being has different capabilities, strengths and weaknesses, you might not be good at something but excellent at other thing. Best available way to come out of comparison is set you goal and just keep working on it, a man on action never has time to compare or complaint.

Accept yourself – remember you are not your LOOKS.

Like I wasted so many years of my life only and only being concerned about my looks as if like I am nothing but MY LOOKS.

Believe it or not, but your value does not lie in how you look but rather what you think and how you conduct yourself in life, start appreciating yourself genuinely and be grateful to God for everything you have and you will find others doing the same.

Negative thought patterns and beliefs about yourself

We keep carrying our negative thought patterns & beliefs about ourselves like I am not good, I am not worthy, I am not deserving, and I can't do this and so many.

Thoughts are powerful as they are a self-rotating cycles. What you think about yourself determines how you feel and how you behave. When you think that you are not deserving, you feel like you are not deserving and you take actions from that being only and then you attempt something with belief that you do not deserve this and ultimately when you fail your belief gets reinforced that YOU ARE NOT DESERVING – now can you see what needs to be changed in this whole cycle – your thought.

Quantum physics has already proved this that our body is made up of infinite number of cells and every cell has its own energy and when we have a negative thought about our self, it gets transferred to nucleus of every cell present in our body and then every cell emits energy adjacent to that thought which means that the energy of that one negative thought gets multiplied and generates so much of negative energy in our body – so be watchful of your thoughts. Be present.

Let go of negative visualization.

Visualization is multiple times powerful than thoughts but unfortunately our mind cannot differentiate between positive or negative visualization – it immediately starts working getting in coherence with the universe for its manifestation. We all do knowingly or unknowingly, the negative visualization ie thinking with emotions the incidents like a loss, fight, argument, embarrassment, failure, insult, rejection and all these pulls down your self-esteem, your confidence and your love for yourself. We cannot stop this but what we can start practicing is being present to what we are doing with this amazing power of our mind and if we get into any negative visualization, replace it with gratitude or affirmations like "Thankyou universe for having me working on this new business idea, as I have full faith that I will crack this" Or start visualizing how you will feel if you gets the desired outcome of whatever you are into and then feel the emotion of that moment.

Acknowledge your fears & trust your decisions.

Do not resist your fears as resisting them will only make them persistent. Rather just acknowledge them by saying "Yes, I know I am little afraid of this, but it is completely Ok to be scared or afraid or nervous, but this will not stop me from doing what I am supposed to do here in this moment". Believe me, even the most powerful or successful people gets afraid or nervous but what makes an ordinary person extra-ordinary is the courage to act in-spite of being scared or afraid of situation. If you are scared of talking to people, just sit down – take few deep breaths and say to yourself "I know I am afraid but I will still attempt talking to people because there is a good news that no matter what happens I will still be alive". Don't be scared of rejection or somebody saying NO to you, just celebrate your attempt and pat on your back.

And trust your decisions – there are no bad or good decisions in life – we take decisions and then we work hard to make them the good ones and vice versa. So just take decisions and give your best to make them right and even if they don't turn right, embrace your choice and move on.

It is OK to make mistakes.

This is all about our conditioning since birth. All through our age we have been told that we should not commit mistakes while in actual life you just cannot succeed without making mistakes but what is more important is learning from them and moving ahead. Accept this fact whole heartedly that we are human beings and we are bound to make mistakes so don't be hard on yourself if you have done anything wrong, just accept it and take responsibility, just do not get into that self-beating mode thinking you are of no worth, you do not know anything and please for god sake do not ask yourself this question: How can I do this mistake?

When you allow yourself space to make mistakes your chances of learning grows exponentially and you don't need a God's person to tell that the more you learn the more you get experienced the more you have possibilities of being successful.

Be Bold / Start speaking in Public.

As far I know and many other wonderful authors and successful people have mentioned on various mediums and shared through books that one of the most powerful known ways for a person to increase his confidence and self-esteem is to be expressive among people and in public. One of the biggest fear among people is of talking to people or connecting to people and when you speak in public your likeability quotient towards yourself shoots and it gives a high to your self-concept and all this helps you starts seeing yourself as a much more worthy and competitive person which expands your self-love.

Now, I know that speaking in public is not an easy task and it takes lot of courage and confidence but if you are determined to cause it for yourself then there are many wonderful platforms today which helps you improve your public speaking skills example Toastmasters Club. Public speaking not only helps you become a better speaker but it also helps you almost in every sphere of life be it your job, be it your presence in any group or social gathering because wherever you go one thing is common and ie People, people and people and when you have confidence of speaking your mind out and expressing what you want to say, you feel decompressed and light inside and thus be able to leaves your mark everywhere.

Start associating with people who trust you and believe in you.

Leave your couches and be out with good people, people who trust you, empowers you and believe in you more than you do. Hold tight and care for the people who allow you to be yourself and allow you to be wrong and then gives you access to grow or expand.

Let go of Toxic people.

Though I believe that every human being is amazing but the hard fact that we all have some toxic relationships or people in our lives, who brings lot of unhealthy criticism, toxic talks and unproductive discussions and I don't know for what we keep holding them. Trust me, letting such people go nowhere means that you do not value people, because your first responsibility is to value and respect your vibes, your mental space and your life and if somebody causing lot of negative space around you, please make distance from them and this is as important as associating with good people.

Practice being grateful or Gratitude

One of the most powerful techniques I have come across in my life to attract positives, be happy and contented and expand your mental space is to practice gratitude. We all have our own problems in life but how long tough times will stay and what impact it will have on us depends what we see ie whether we see the problems & challenges or we see the good things available in our lives and the possibilities available to cause so many things. Right from getting out of your bed in morning till going back to you bed in night, we can be grateful to so many things but as human beings we have this mental conditioning to only and only see that black spot on the white board and not the whole clean space it has. We can be grateful in any situation if we can develop this ability in our-self and the formula of Gratitude simply works like whatever you feel grateful for, whatever you acknowledges multiplies and comes back to you in abundance, considering the emotion is genuine.

Affirmations

Life doesn't works on logic but magic and magic happens only for those who have faith and belief.

Writing affirmations is also one such magic where you consider the desired state is already here and then you write gratitude for that state feeling it and feeling it in a way like it is now and true in present moment. For example, if you are working on to improve your self-love then you may write "Thankyou universe for making me a person in love with myself". Affirmations are so so powerful that it can change your mental state and thus the outcome. Try this next time when you are about to enter any meeting or interview or sales presentation thanking universe for the success in that meeting and feel the difference in your confidence.

You may start by simply taking on this practice of saying multiple times to yourself in day "I like myself, I like myself, I like myself", say this to yourself with your eyes closed and you will feel an energy running down your whole body.

Exercise, meditate, recharge yourself

Very important to take out time for recharging yourself as only healthy body contains a healthy mind and a healthy spirit. Practice some yoga or meditation, take a walk, go to gym as this will help you connect with yourself having some me time.

Do completion with your past

One big area of concern and as I took so many years of my life to recognize that It was not me but rather that incident which was driving my life, because of that I could not see so many possibilities I could have worked on and changed my life but I am grateful that I got the opportunity of seeing this before leaving this world. Invite you here to check if there is any such incident, mistake of yours or any other event which has kept you hooked still to your past and filled with inhibitions, complexes and you have been hard on yourself due to that – if yes, please accept that whatever happened and what you have been telling yourself since then are two different things – what happened, just happened and its past now so please complete with it, if required please forgive yourself or even someone else and take the responsibility of your future and no one else can do this for you as the saying goes "If it is to be, it is up to me".

Judge your efforts and not the result

One big reason of self-beating is the system of this society or world as only results are recognized, but be your own judge and celebrate your efforts. Do not judge yourself for the result but rather the efforts you have put into as the result can vary depending on many factors and sometimes can be out of your control, but what is under your control is your efforts, so isn't it fair to asses on it.

Write down your goods / positives

Tough to do believe me but magical on impact. Sit down with a pen and paper and write down your good things and positive habits or traits and then start working on them to strengthen them.

This practice will really put you on surprise as when you write it down it gives you good feeling knowing how any good things you are carrying into you.

Do things that makes you happy

Do things what makes you happy, it can be dance, party with your friends, going to movie over the weekend, shopping, reading books, going for a vacation, taking your parents out or even being on bed whole day lethargically. Purpose is to do what you like.

Reward yourself for accomplishments

Last but not the least, celebrate your smalls or big accomplishments. Never ever allow your mind to make you victim of imposter syndrome which gives you doubt of being a doer or achiever even when you are recognized for something, so be the first one to celebrate.

I can vouch for this, following even if not all but some of these practices will bring a drastic difference in degree of your love for yourself and will also boost your confidence, self-esteem and your perceptions and judgements about yourself and you will become more effective in almost every sphere of your life. These practices will alter your listening about yourself & it will change the way you have been relating yourself to. Communication with your own self is the most important communication in world and these practices will improve and upgrade the quality of this communication in your life which will transform things.

All the best and wish you all good health and success.

Conclusion

Words are not just words but the energy transferred in form of language and your Words owns the power to either transform or damage the lives of yourself or others. We all have been told since our childhood by our parents or elders to always speak carefully and wisely.

Unfortunately, we all only know this but do not implement into our lives. Very less often, we remain diligent of our words, the words we speak to others and the words we speak to ourselves. And this ignorance acts as Culprit of destroying so many lives, as words are used with no care and they damage or harm people's esteem, confidence, respect and belief badly and make them become someone really distant from what they dreams of or aspires to be. To make someone lose, you actually do not need to do anything big, just take away that person's love and respect for himself and rest will be done by that person himself only and this is what our words are capable of doing. Words have power to transform the communities, nations and whole world if used with love and compassion as purpose, but something not practiced really in practical world. Sometimes, few words when just used without being careful leaves such marks on one's identity and character, leaving that person living his remaining whole life from that belief only and takes away all his freedom of being someone who he has always been capable of actually.

Life after a passing remark is also about one such incident from my very own life, wherein one passing remark from one of my relative changed me and my life upside down. Surprisingly for that person, it was just a passing remark and no surprise that even for his whole life, he shall ever be aware of what his one passing remark did to a teenager who at an age of fifteen was about to enter into the most critical phase of his life where he would have planned to do, to attempt so any things personally and professionally but that one day took away everything from me and I carried that remark and its burden on my mind for so long. This story is about how it altered my identity altogether and impacted every single aspect of my life be it career, relationships, intimacy, my self-expression or my physical & mental health. Every human being carries their physical, mental and emotional reserves and the amount of these reserves proves to be really crucial in determining how far you goes in life and this book is about how an incident emptied by reserves and I only kept struggling to refill them.

But then even the longest nights are followed by mornings and so does life teaches us to keep moving and keep finding the end of the dark tunnel where in there will be light and way forward and in my life, this long tunnel starts approaching its end when I met beautiful souls and they started filing my void with love and their belief in myself. Good people are like fragrances, wherever they travel makes the environment beautiful.

Love you all my readers – Stay happy, stay blessed, stay grateful and stay in LOVE WITH YOURSELF.

www.ingramcontent.com/pod-product-compliance
Lightning Source LLC
LaVergne TN
LVHW041532070526
838199LV00046B/1630